Lc. Culminant 'La Tuilerie,' a mericlone flowering for the first time.

YOU CAN GROW
CATTLEYA
ORCHIDS

By MARY NOBLE

A SEQUEL TO

YOU CAN GROW ORCHIDS

Drawings by
MARION RUFF SHEEHAN

Published by:
Mary Noble McQuerry, Jacksonville Florida

Copyright © 1968
By MARY NOBLE

Printed in the United States of America
First edition

Second Printing 1977

Third Printing 1980

ISBN 0-913928-02-X

All rights reserved. This book, or any part thereof, may not be reproduced in any form without written permission from the author who is also the publisher. This includes the making of copies by any photo process, or by any electronic or mechanical device, printed or written or oral, or recording for sound or visual reproduction or for use in any knowledge retrieval system or device, unless permission in writing is obtained from the copyright proprietor.

CONTENTS

Dedicated with affection to
MR. AND MRS. RODNEY WILCOX JONES

Rodney Wilcox Jones always wears an orchid boutonniere and carries a box of small flowers along on a trip.

The Jones have an extensive orchid collection at their home in New Rochelle, N. Y.

When I was a beginning orchidist, Rodney Wilcox Jones became President of the American Orchid Society (1942-1948). I was enchanted by "Notes from Broadview" which he wrote about his own orchids for the AOS Bulletin.

So, one Sunday afternoon when I was vacationing in New York, I took the train up to New Rochelle, rang the doorbell at 100 Broadview Avenue and asked to see the orchids. I was afraid the President of AOS would be too busy to bother with an unknown novice orchid grower, but the Jones family received me with their typical warmth and courtesy and we have been friends ever since.

My experience is only one of many, as Rodney and Charlotte have done more than any other two people to make friends for orchids. They have traveled all over the world visiting orchid growers. Rodney has given innumerable programs for orchid societies around the globe, and they have encouraged many people in many places to share this fascinating hobby.

Dedicating this book to Rod and Lotta is just my way of saying "thank you" for all of us.

M. N.

YOUR INTRODUCTION TO CATTLEYAS

Cattleyas are the "orchid orchids," the ones most grown, most worn, most often thought of when the word "orchid" is mentioned.

If your collection is a conglomeration, cattleyas are probably in the majority. Fortunately, they are compatible with many other types of orchids. If you have just bought your first orchid, chances are it is of the cattleya type.

When you have seen one cattleya, you have not seen them all. Purple cattleyas are numerous, but they are varied as well. They come in light, dark and intermediate shades. But besides purple, cattleyas and their hybrids bloom in glistening white, vibrant yellow, glowing red, and cool lime green, among others. Some are combinations of colors, some have spots.

Sizes and shapes are just as diverse. There are bigger and bigger hybrids, more and more exotic cluster types in smaller sizes, and many charming novelties that cannot be lumped into any general descriptions.

This book is a sequel to YOU CAN GROW ORCHIDS and I hope you have read that book for a basic knowledge of orchid culture and information about types other than the cattleya clan. You may find a bit of repetition here, but the first book was general. This one, by its concentration, is more detailed and supplements the introductory book.

When I say CATTLEYA in the title, I consider the broad spectrum. I include several genera allied to the genus Cattleya and hybridized with it, for the flowers classed as cattleyas may be combinations of two, three or four genera. Laelias, epidendrums, sophronitis, brassavolas and others have a place here because they have been bred with cattleyas and are similar in their structure and culture.

To date there are 24 compound genera which include Cattleya, with more being registered all the time. The most familiar compounds are Laeliocattleya (two genera) and Brassolaeliocattleya (three genera). But you will be hearing more about such conglomerates as Yamadara (Cattleya x Brassavola x Laelia x Epidendrum.) Don't be alarmed. You'll get accustomed to their names.

Even so, I can only begin to mention the species (more than 50 Cattleyas), and barely touch on the hybrids of which there are thousands. I refer you to the hybrid lists (see book list) and nursery catalogs for parentage and descriptions of plants that interest you. I suggest you visit orchid shows and orchid nurseries in your area and as you travel to see the forever new crop of orchid debutantes in this group. Orchids don't stand still. There are always new flowers to enchant you.

The idea of a series of orchid paperbacks is not original with this author. James Veitch and Sons, English nurserymen, published A Manual of Orchidaceous Plants in 10 parts between 1887 and 1894. There was one general volume, and nine on specialized groups. Now reprinted in hard covers, Veitch's Manual is still a valuable reference to the species.

So, my aim in this second volume of my series is to give you an understanding of the cattleyas and their allies so you can choose wisely, grow your plants well, and enjoy your flowers. Good luck!

M. N.

CHAPTER I

THE PLANT
AND ITS HABITS

Take a mature cattleya plant. If you understand how it is put together and how it grows, you will understand how to take care of it according to its cycles of growth.

Pronounce the name "KAT-lee-a" or "CAT-lee-uh." For the origin of the name see Chapter IV.

Unifoliate Cattleyas

A cattleya plant has roots, stems, leaves and flowers just like any other plant. The size, shape and arrangement of these parts varies according to the species. But in the usual unifoliate cattleya hybrid grown today a mature plant looks like this. Refer to the sketch, and to a live plant to become familiar with the parts.

PSEUDOBULB — The plant has several upright green growths each about eight or nine inches high growing parallel to each other. These are somewhat wider in the middle than at the top and bottom and run an inch or more in width at the widest point and about as big around as a pencil at the narrowest point at the base or ankle. These growths are called pseudobulbs and spoken of as "bulbs." "Pseudo" means false and they are not bulbs. Technically they are branches, but they grow upright rather than horizontal, which is the usual pattern of branches on shrubs and trees. The pseudobulbs are storage organs for water and food. Pronunciation: "SUE-doe-bulb."

LEAF — On top of each pseudobulb is a single leaf that may be 12 inches long and two or three inches wide at the widest part. It is green and thick like leather, and has a single midrib the length of the center. You can see veins in the leaf if you hold it up to the light.

At the bottom the sides of the leaf are almost folded together at the top of the bulb. The leaf may stand straight up or arch backwards. While it is growing, it is folded flat through the middle.

A single leaf characterizes a cattleya of the unifoliate type. "Unifoliate" means "one leaf" and indicates one leaf per bulb. Bifoliate cattleyas are described later in this chapter.

While the pseudobulb is growing it has a thin green covering in layers, additional layers showing as it grows. This covering turns brown and feels like tissue paper when the bulb is mature. The top of the last of these green (later brown) covers is just below the point where bulb and leaf join.

Technically, this outer wrapping consists of eight leaves, but the ninth one on top of the bulb is the only one that stays green and functions like a leaf. That it, it makes starch and sugar for growth by a process known as photosynthesis. The other eight leaves are never called leaves. They are sometimes alluded to as sheathing leaves, which is confusing with the flower sheath. I prefer to call them sarongs because they wrap tightly around the curvaceous bulbs.

Do not remove the sarongs until they turn brown and dry indicating that their protective work is done, and take care not to injure the eyes which are beneath them.

SHEATH — Rising from the point where bulb and leaf join is a green sheath perhaps four inches high and an inch or so wide. It is shaped like a broad knife blade and grows at a slight angle so there is space between it and the leaf. It develops as the pseudobulb develops and when the leaf unfolds, the top of the sheath is generally visible.

The flower sheath is of thinner green tissue than the leaf. Flower buds push up inside this sheath and when they emerge from the top of it they are about half developed. The sheath has a silky, silvery lining. Some cattleyas have double sheaths, one within the other.

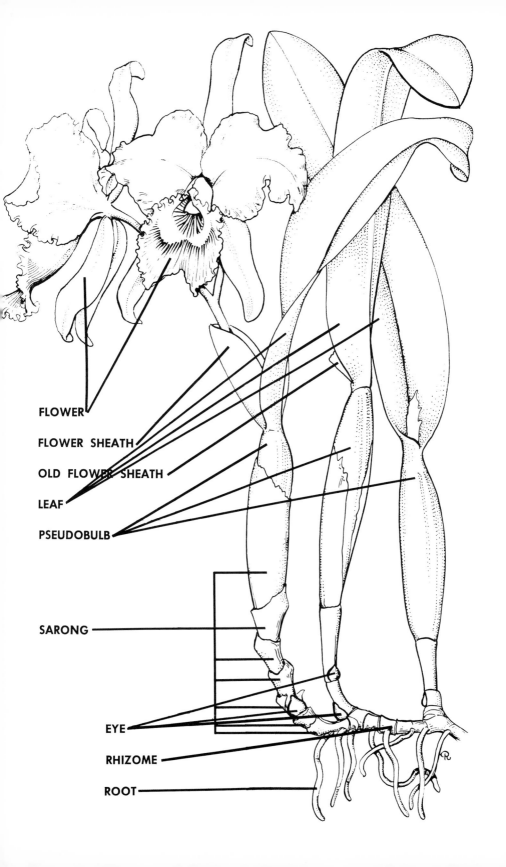

FLOWER

FLOWER SHEATH

OLD FLOWER SHEATH

LEAF

PSEUDOBULB

SARONG

EYE

RHIZOME

ROOT

Sometimes the sheath turns brown, which may be normal or not. More of this later.

Seedlings rarely make sheaths. If a full-grown plant matures its bulb and leaf without producing a sheath the growth is called "blind." It may bloom anyhow. A weak bulb of a poorly grown plant may be blind.

RHIZOME — The five or six bulbs of this typical plant (more or less) are connected by a brown stem that creeps along the top of the potting material and may run for an inch between each bulb. This woody stem from which the bulbs branch is comparable to the trunk of a woody shrub except that it grows horizontally rather than vertically.

This connecting link, actually the main stem, is called a rhizome ("RYE-zom" rhymes with "home.") It may be long or short depending on the plant's habit and heredity.

So now you see that our cattleya orchid has all the same parts as a woody shrub in your garden, but is like you trimmed off one whole side of the shrub and laid it on the ground with the trunk along the top of the soil. This would make the branches point upward (as do the pseudo-bulbs), and the trunk extend horizontally (as does the rhizome.)

ROOTS — There are roots, of course, which grow from the base of the bulb which becomes the rhizome. New roots are white with green tips and they stick tenaciously to whatever surface they encounter because in nature this is how orchids hold themselves onto trees and rocks.

Roots appear at different times in the cycle of plant growth depending on the ancestry of the plant, if a hybrid, or its natural cycle if a species. More of this in the chapter on Potting.

Old roots look dirty, brown and lifeless but don't be deceived. They are more useful than they look. See Potting.

FLOWERS — If a plant is of mature size and is well grown, each pseudobulb produces flowers when conditions are right. Once a pseudobulb has flowered, it will not bloom again.

Failure to flower may be due to poor culture, insufficient light or other environmental factors. See chapter on Problems. The timing of flowering varies with the species and their hybrids and is discussed later in this chapter. Do not get excited if a sheath appears and has no flowers immediately, that may be its nature. But once a bulb flowers, do not expect more blooms on that plant until it makes a new bulb, leaf and sheath unless there were two or more new bulbs produced in that growth cycle.

EYE — At the base of each bulb just above the rhizome you can see a small green triangular bump. This is called an eye. There are generally three eyes on each bulb.

The eye is the vegetative bud. Each of the three is located above a circular joint or ring on the bulb, which botanically locates it in the axil of the sarong (a leaf) which was attached at this point to the stem (bulb.) But you can't see the eye until you remove the brown sarong. If you don't remove the sarong, the eye will push through it when it gets ready to grow.

The largest eye is about one-half inch high. The other two are slightly stair-stepped, one on the other side of the bulb and a tiny one one step up above the major eye.

When it is time for the plant to grow this eye will begin to swell and will, in time, become another complete bulb, leaf, sheath with roots and flowers like the bulb to which it is now attached. While it is growing it is called a lead.

If you grow your plant well, two eyes on opposite sides of a bulb may grow at once but the third and highest one rarely develops unless misfortune befalls the others. It may grow later to activate a back bulb. See Propagation chapter. If a plant has been infested with scale, the eyes may be brown and lifeless and unable to grow. See Problem chapter.

The type of growth described above is called sympodial ("sim-PO-dee-al.") It is a type of growth that is repetitious, as each new shoot develops into a bulb that is potentially a flowering growth. The plant moves sideways as it grows.

OLD BULBS — Bulbs that have flowered support the newer bulbs and their flowers. A normal cattleya hybrid plant consists of at least three bulbs plus the new growth. The average is five or six bulbs. Back bulb divisions may originate with two bulbs plus the new lead. Specimen plants may have dozens of bulbs.

Never is one bulb self-sufficient and considered a plant in this group. It is important to have at least three plump bulbs with leaves to support each new lead (growing bulb.)

Laeliocattleya Wine Festival, a cluster type with bronze and purple flowers.

An old bulb retains its leaf for about five years under congenial conditions. When it is finished the leaf turns yellow and falls off, breaking cleanly at the point where it joins the bulb. Let it fall naturally. If you try to force it you may tear the tissue of the bulb. Leaves that turn brown at the front of the plant may be disabled by insects or disease. Plants must have leaves to manufacture food, but do not be alarmed if leaves at the back of the plant drop.

Old bulbs may become wrinkled, vertically, as the front growing part of the plant draws on their supplies of food and moisture. If bulbs become wrinkled and shriveled when fairly new, there is a problem.

Bifoliate Cattleyas

What we have just described is a typical unifoliate cattleya plant with one leaf per bulb. It may be a species or a hybrid.

Another group of cattleyas is the bifoliate type, meaning "two leaves" per bulb.

These cattleyas are sometimes called "cluster type" because they may have several flowers to a stem, but not all of them do. The flowers are generally smaller than those of the unifoliate type.

The appearance of the plants is somewhat modified, but the basic parts are the same.

Aside from having two or three leaves at the top of each pseudobulb, the leaves of the bifoliate type are generally shorter and more rounded than the unifoliates, and are inclined to lay flatter at right angles from the bulbs. If there is a third leaf it is below the top pair.

Bulbs of the bifoliates may be flatter or thinner, taller or shorter than the unifoliate bulbs. Some of the bifoliate plants are quite diminutive. Others are giants. Cattleya guttata may have pencil slim bulbs three feet high.

Plants which are hybrids with both unifoliate and bifoliate species in their ancestry may have one or more leaves per bulb varying from bulb to bulb.

Other Plants in the Alliance

In our broad grouping of the Cattleya Alliance, most of the plants in the other genera follow the same pattern of growth and have the same plant parts although sizes and shapes are diverse. (See sketches page 16.)

Laelias may be very large or very small plants. Sophronitis are dainty and schomburgkias are enormous by comparison. Some brassavolas have round leaves like pencils.

Epidendrums are divided into the bulbous types with growth in the cattleya pattern but bulbs are frequently egg-shaped, and the reed stem epidendrums which have no pseudobulbs but are monopodial and grow upwards. Their pencil-slim stems are very tall and have small leaves along their lengths. These epis make offsets readily and generally there are dozens of plants in a clump.

Hybrids between the genera vary greatly in size and shape according to their ancestry.

The Growth Cycle

Each pseudobulb, if well grown, has everything . . . stem, leaf, roots, and flowers. It is like a cake mix. All you do is add the ingredients of water, air, sunshine and fertilizer.

Consider the growth cycle of a typical unifoliate plant. Assume it is a Cattleya mossiae, a spring-blooming species. This plant flowers near Easter, and it used to be the major cut flower for the spring market but now modern hybrids (many with C. mossiae in their ancestry) of superior form and color have largely supplanted it.

However, let's use it for an example. Shortly after it blooms in the spring an eye at the base of the bulb that just bloomed begins to swell. It grows forward parallel with the rhizome for a couple of inches, then turns its pointed tip upwards. From then on the lead grows beside and parallel to the pseudobulb that just flowered.

The lead keeps going until it has formed another pseudobulb. The bulb is inclined to be thin while growing, fattening up as it matures. The leaf is folded together at the top, but in time the distinction can be made between leaf and bulb, and when the leaf unfolds the top of the sheath should be visible.

◀ **Plant habits. Top left, Cattleya skinneri. Top right, Sophronitis coccinea (grandiflora). Lower left, Laelia harpophylla. Lower right, Brassavola digbyana.**

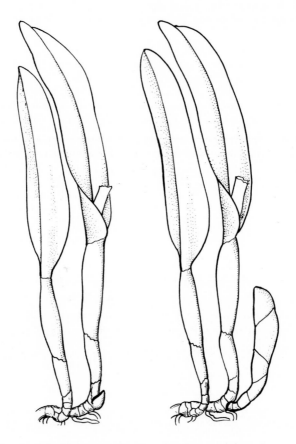

New eye begins to swell. New lead turns upward.

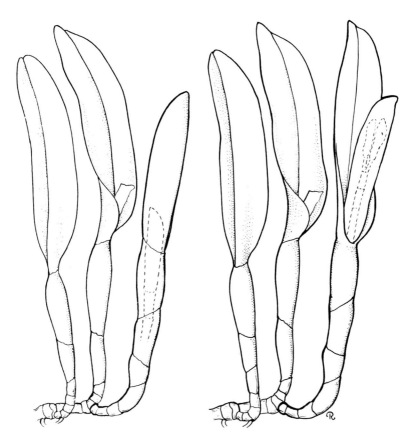

Leaf is folded as growth elongates. Sheath forms. Bulb is mature. Flowers appear in sheath.

This lead generally produces new roots from its base when the growth is partially developed.

By the end of summer the new bulb, leaf, and sheath are completed and roots are in the pot. Then nothing visible happens all winter. Sometime during the short days of winter the flower buds begin to develop and by early spring they can be seen in the sheath. By this time the flower sheath may be brown, and the sarongs may be brown and dry, too.

If the Cattleya mossiae plant produced more than one new lead and pseudobulb during the previous summer, all of these new bulbs produce flowers at one time, then set about at once making new vegetative growths which will advance all summer and rest all winter.

Another pattern of behavior is typical of Cattleya warscewiczii (Cattleya gigas.) A plant in this group begins to grow in winter or early spring. The pseudobulb develops rapidly and by the time the leaf unfolds there may be buds in the sheath. The blooms may open even before the bulb has finished growing. Roots may appear with the flowers, or before or after. Then the plant does nothing until the following winter when it begins to grow again.

Plants of this type may make second growths right after the first round, which should flower right away but may be blind because the summer night temperature is too high for flower development.

If a large plant in this category makes several bulbs simultaneously, they may not necessarily flower together but each one as it reaches a certain stage of development. Whereas in the C. mossiae group that sits before flowering, all the bulbs on a plant bloom together because they have been dormant and the trigger that starts the buds developing goes off in all the bulbs at once.

Modern hybrids are so complex in their inheritance that few of them fall into these two definite categories. Therefore, a hybrid may make up a bulb and rest before flowering, or it may bloom on new growth at once. It may begin a new lead before or during flowering, or it may make several new bulbs at once.

You can only learn the habits of your plants as individuals, and treat them according to their stages of development. Some hybrids bloom twice in a year, some three times in two years. Some take very little rest between producing new leads. Others maintain a dependable pattern year after year. More on this in Heredity chapter.

How to Buy Plants

Orchids of the cattleya type are generally sold by pot sizes. A 5-inch or 6-inch pot should be flowering size. A plant may bloom at 3-inch or 4-inch if its heredity keeps it small. Check for sheaths and ask specifically for flowering size plants.

SEEDLINGS—Seedling plants are offered in flasks, community pots of small plants all of one kind, and individual pots from thumb pot size on up. How long it takes to reach flowering size depends upon the conditions and care you can provide and its heredity which determines the size of the mature growth.

If you are new at orchids, don't buy small seedlings or flasks. Seedlings are babies and more tender than tough old adult plants and besides, you may run out of interest or patience before they ever bloom. Buy mature plants in bloom so you can see what you are getting. When

Epidendrum pseudepidendrum, a curious flower of green and orange.

you build up your collection so you have plants in bloom successively. then add some seedlings that are near blooming size and grow them on. There's fun in seeing a seedling bloom for the first time because of the great variability in the hybrids. You might have the choice one of the litter.

DIVISIONS — Divisions are of two types. Large mature plants that have produced enough bulbs to be divided into two or more plants, each with good eyes or new leads and supporting bulbs. Divisions with leads or eyes on current bulbs are called front divisions and should grow and bloom without interruption. See Propagation chapter.

BACK BULBS — Back bulbs are the old, inactive bulbs with green eyes visible but on bulbs that bloomed several seasons ago. If there is at least one good eye and one or two leaves, two or three back bulbs may be cut off into a division and induced to grow. This is a method of propagating fine plants, but is slower than a front division as generally the first bulb will be small and blind and it may take two or three years to grow normal size flowering bulbs. Back bulbs of average plants are discarded when repotting to reduce pot size, but back bulbs of fine plants may be offered for sale at reasonable prices.

MERICLONES — These are plants produced by a technical process of cell division and are vegetative divisions of their mother plants. Mericlones are grown like seedlings in flasks, community pots and individual pots. Whereas seedlings are variable within the population from one seed pod, mericlones are of known quality because of being identical. Therefore, prices for some mericlones are higher than for some seedlings of the same size. More on this in Propagation chapter.

Already you have come to some unfamiliar words that will become part of your orchid vocabulary. If you are not sure of the meaning, consult the glossary (page 135) as you read, and refer to it when you come to a new word like you turn to the cast of characters in the front of a paperback mystery novel to become familiar with them as they enter the story.

CHAPTER II

ENVIRONMENT AND TENDER LOVING CARE

Among the plants of the tropics orchids are relatively small, so they do not inhabit the dense jungle undergrowth where the competition would overpower them. Instead they seek out open spaces. They grow high in the trees, as cliff-hangers near waterfalls or rivers, even on rocks by the sea in order to get their share of light, moisture and air.

Generally cattleyas and their related clans are classed as epiphytes but some are lithophytes or rupicolous plants that grow on the rocks.

Epiphytes (pronounced "EP-e-fights") grow on other plants without harming their hosts. They are not parasites.

Orchids derive their nourishment from air, bits of bird manure and humus that collect in crevices of the tree bark or rock, and moisture from rain, dew and fog.

They grow in company with bromeliads, ferns, mosses, and lichens.

The orchids we are considering in this book are all native to tropical America but each species has definite localized habitats.

Fifty species of Cattleya are recognized. Most of them are native to Brazil but range along the north coast of South America, in the Andes, and up into Central America.

Epidendrums, for instance, also grow wild in the Caribbean, and Florida.

Laelia Icarus is orange. (L. cinnabarina x L. flava.)

Tropical climates generally have distinct wet and dry seasons. Orchids with pseudobulbs are equipped to store up reserves of food and moisture during the warm wet seasons to tide them over the cool dry periods. Some of them need the drought and cold to mature their growths and develop flowers. But even in the tropical dry seasons there are fogs, clouds and dew to provide moisture, especially at high altitudes where many of them grow. Many orchids bathe in mists from rivers, streams and waterfalls.

And do not think all orchids are hot climate plants. If you have been in the tropics you know that at some altitudes the nights can be frigid.

Orchids don't have it easy in nature. They have to be tough to survive. But if you understand their needs and supply same, they should grow and flower at maximum capacity.

LOCATION: Your facilities may be extensive or modest. A greenhouse is the best enclosure for providing optimum environment with the least trouble. Many prefabricated models are available in all sorts of shapes, sizes and prices.

Many people grow orchids in their homes. An exposure that receives morning sun is desirable.

Many people grow orchids with success in windowless rooms such as basements by using artificial lights. People in apartments use plant carts with lights for small collections.

In warm climates many people grow orchids outdoors swinging from tree limbs or beneath trellises or shade houses in the garden.

Most of the problem with indoor growing is that of providing enough light and humidity but if you understand what the plants need, you can attempt to adjust the environment accordingly.

Cattleya aclandiae, a species. The flower is olive green blotched with dark purple, the lip and the column magenta.

What Orchids Need

The elements of the environment to consider are light and shade including the length of the day; temperature and air circulation; water and humidity; and nutrients. Potting materials are discussed in another chapter.

All the environmental factors are interrelated. If you have higher temperature you need brighter light and higher humidity. If plants are in open spaces where breezes are brisk you need more water and humidity to offset excessive evaporation. If sunlight is scarce on dull winter days, lowering the temperature and decreasing the humidity will help to balance the atmosphere.

Photosynthesis and Respiration

Two processes maintain plant life, and to understand your plants you need to know what goes on inside them.

PHOTOSYNTHESIS — This is a process upon which all life in the world depends. It occurs only in green parts of plants, the cells which contain chlorophyll.

Photosynthesis (pronounce just like it looks with accent on "sin") means "manufacture by light" and is the name of the process by which living green cells in plants make sugar (glucose), starch and other compounds during the day from carbon, hydrogen and oxygen derived from water and carbon dioxide.

These accumulate, are moved around inside the plants at night, and are transformed into materials for new tissues and growth.

Sunlight (or artificial light) provides the energy for photosynthesis. It ceases in darkness and thus most growth actually takes place at night when the materials are being converted from sugar into other compounds.

RESPIRATION — A process called respiration breaks down the sugars and starches. It takes place constantly in all cells, not only the green ones, and regardless of whether it is day or night.

Surplus oxygen and water vapor left over after respiration are given off into the air by the leaves. All the oxygen in the air we breathe is provided by green leaves (either on land or phytoplankton in the ocean.)

YOUR PLANTS — You must provide your plants with suitable conditions for efficient conduct of photosynthesis. This means adequate light and suitable temperature, both of proper duration, so that the plants can produce enough sugar to keep themselves alive and growing. But more than that, you must help them, by the proper environment, to make more than enough sugar to stay alive. They need surplus to grow and to produce flowers.

Since respiration goes on day and night and is not affected by light, temperature comes into the picture.

You want sufficient respiration for plant activity, but it should be at a lesser rate than photosynthesis. This way, the plants are able to store reserves produced by photosynthesis and not lost by respiration, and these reserves are used for maximum growth and such extras as flower and seed production.

You can help your plants to operate these two processes with the greatest efficiency by providing or regulating the environmental factors which are concerned. Of course, all of this is overly simplified, but I'm no chemist, and probably you are not either.

Light and Shade

Light from the sun is the energy that runs the manufacturing process in the plant during the day.

Light in the morning to start up the machinery is important, hence specifications for placing a greenhouse where it gets morning sun, if not all day, or for growing plants in an east or south window.

The recommended range for the cattleya group is 3,000 to 3,500 foot candles. They will grow and bloom from upwards of 1,000 or 2,000 foot candles, and can probably stand up to 12,000 or so IF the leaf temperature is kept cool.

You can measure foot candles with a photographic light meter or with one made by General Electric that indicates foot candles. When you are experienced you recognize plants which are yellow or sunburned as getting too much light and those that are too deep a green with floppy growths as being too shaded.

An overabundance of light does not hasten photosynthesis as there is a saturation point of greatest efficiency beyond which the plants cannot use the extra light.

But plants can stand and can use extra light if other factors are in proportion. If humidity and air movement are heightened enough to keep leaf tissues cool, greater light is possible. Leaf temperature and air temperature are not the same and if a leaf feels warm to your touch either decrease the light or raise the humidity and circulation to prevent it from burning.

The light reading in the greenhouse aisle is not the same for all plants. Plants receive varying amounts of light depending on the location on the bench, shade from overhead or neighboring plants, even the shade of one leaf on another. Leaf position is another factor in whether or not the sunlight is penetrating it at greatest capacity. And since the leaves on orchids tend to curve in different directions, only an average reading can be taken.

You can increase the light, if needed, by painting wood surfaces inside the greenhouse white, even the edges of the benches. Marble chips on the ground reflect light. Windowsillers who don't want to paint their sills to reflect might put opaque white plastic over the surrounding surfaces for reflection.

The duration of the light, called daylength, controls the development of flower buds in some species and their hybrids. Some plants produce buds when days are short and others when days are long. If this character is known the plants are called "controllable" and it is possible to manipulate the daylength to bring flowers into bloom for holidays. See Chapter III.

Plants grown in your home may be influenced by the electric lights in the room. If they need short days to set buds and you burn lights in the evenings, they may not bloom.

Brassavola nodosa has a white lip and pale green sepals and petals. Note the curious terete foliage.

Brassocattleya Binosa 'Polka Dot' is B. nodosa x Cattleya bicolor.

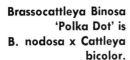

Locating your greenhouse so it gets the most light available is important and also the direction in which it runs if you live in northern latitudes. Build your house where there is too much sun, if possible, because you can always shade it, but if the location is continuously shaded by trees or buildings, it is difficult to increase the light.

Saran screen, hi-rib expanded metal (a plasterer's lath), and other shade materials may be used to filter the light on an open structure.

Light intensity and direction change all day long and from day to day according to the clouds and the seasons. The ideal maximum may be achieved only briefly as the sun passses overhead. In places where there are cumulus clouds, where there is smog, or where soot coats the glass, light intensity is reduced.

The best you can do in any situation is to achieve a desirable range to which your plants respond by growing and blooming.

ARTIFICIAL LIGHTS — General recommendations call for the use of Gro-Lux fluorescent lights with one incandescent 25-watt bulb added for every four tubes (equalling 10 to 20 percent of the total wattage.) Or you can use wide-spectrum Gro-Lux lights.

Mount the lights under reflectors directly above the plants and about three inches apart. Control them with an automatic switch to run 14 to 16 hours per day.

Artificial lights may be used along with daylight to supplement it in places where there are numerous dull days or where smog obscures the sun. Lights hasten the growth of seedlings (see Propagation chapter) and make it possible to use spaces indoors, beneath the greenhouse benches (if air is warm enough), or even to grow plants in basements. A delightful New Orleans custom is that of making a garden room in the house. It must be possible to maintain some humidity in the room without damaging the furnishings or floor.

Temperature and Circulation

The temperature of the areas where these orchids grow native is quite variable and may run to extremes. For instance, Cattleya warscewiczii grows in the Andes at 7,000 to 8,000 feet elevation and the temperature may fall below freezing at night in the winter or drop from 80 degrees F. to 40 degrees F. during a summer day and night. This is an exception, not recommended for cultivated plants.

Besides, plants that you grow probably have spent their lives in controlled environments from the time their seeds were sown in sterilized bottles and are not accustomed to the vagaries of nature.

Temperature is important to plant growth as plants may survive but not grow above and below certain critical figures.

The desirable range for most cattleyas and their allies is between 63 and 86 degrees F. by day and 55 to 68 degrees F. at night.

In many climates the greenhouse and the outside air rise above 86 degrees F. but plants are happy if humidity cools the air, reduces evaporation and keeps the leaves cool.

Temperature is related to light because plants accumulate heat energy from the light they absorb and then have to get rid of the heat. If the heat that is generated in the plants by the light cannot escape, then it destroys the green chlorophyll and leaves turn yellow and cease photosynthesis.

The temperature of a leaf in bright sun for any length of time is almost always higher than the temperature of the air around it. Heat injury depends on the duration of the exposure. Moving air helps dissipate it.

In a warm climate or on warm days, opening vents at the top of the greenhouse will let the heat escape from the house because hot air rises. If outside air is dry and hot, fans and wet pads may be needed.

If your greenhouse has high sides and roof, and thus room for air to move over and around the plants, heat will not build up so rapidly.

In a cold climate, building up heat may be desirable and it may be well to have the roof barely above the benches to keep the air warm enough. A lining of clear polyethylene film inside the glass in winter will help to keep the air warm and to reduce your fuel bills.

Most orchids can endure lower night temperatures briefly but not consistently. The greatest danger lies in damage to flower buds.

On the other hand, consistently high night temperatures are undesirable because of the respiration process. One orchid grower told me "orchids like to sleep cool" and this is why.

You wish to increase the photosynthesis rate so that it manufactures reserves to be stored for maximum growth and flowering. If respiration goes on at a high rate, it uses up all the sugars and starches as fast as photosynthesis makes them. So the secret is to slow down the respiration without slowing down the growth.

Photosynthesis takes place during the day. Respiration takes place day and night. By slowing down respiration at night when there is no photosynthesis, the compounds manufactured during the day are not all used up.

You can slow down respiration by lowering the temperature at night.

Don't think you are doing your plants a favor to keep them hot at night. Let them cool off but not enough for cold to damage plant tissues or flower buds.

If you are a windowsill grower and your house is hot at night, move the orchids to a room that is cool but not drafty.

In hot climates some orchids will not flower well if the nights consistently are not much different from the days as to temperature. In Singapore, for example, they say some cattleyas do not bloom well. The buds grow rapidly and open quickly but do not have much substance. With more temperature change, there would be more reserve for flower production and buds would develop more slowly as well. Fortunately, the climate in Singapore and similar places is ideal for other types of orchids which grow superbly.

Orchids do not like stagnant air so a slight air movement is desirable if it is not cold. In wintry weather, open a roof vent at the far end of the greenhouse from the heater and air will move through the house, but don't do this if too much cold will come in or if ice will form and prevent you from closing the vent later.

In warm climates cattleyas grown outdoors may get too much moving air. If bulbs shrivel the relationship between the water taken up and that transpired into the breezes is unbalanced. Either provide more humidity or a wind break.

Airconditioning units like we use in our homes dehumidify air, which is desirable for people but not for plants. If used in greenhouses, humidity must be increased to offset the dryness.

Providing extra carbon dioxide in closed greenhouses by burning candles, alcohol, or from compressed gas permits higher light intensity and seems to induce greater growth if other factors are in balance.

Polluted outside air is known to damage orchids, especially flowers.

C. Karae Lyn Sugiyama (C. Joyce Hannington x C. Edithiae).

Water and Humidity

Water is a very important element in plant growth. Not only is it a factor in photosynthesis by supplying hydrogen and oxygen but it is the transportation medium in which nutritional elements move about in the plants. Ninety percent of the weight of an orchid plant is water.

Because of their pseudobulbs and thick leaves, cattleya plants can store up some water for emergency periods, which is what sees them through the dry seasons of the tropical calendar. In many species the rest from growth induced by the dryness, when photosynthesis and respiration are decreased by lack of water, is necessary to the plant's cycle of development. Keeping such plants in vegetative condition generally results in weak growths that do not flower.

Cattleya species have definite adaptation and need for simulation of the wet and dry seasons in their native habitats. This is achieved in cultivation by giving water less often, but watering thoroughly when you do. It does not mean no water at all because you must recall the drift from the waterfall or the moisture from dew and fog.

Cattleya hybrids, by virtue of being hybrids, are more modified in their habits which they inherit from both sides of the family tree. And while some of advanced generations may react like their ancestors, quite often the rest or dry period is very slight. New growth may be developing even while old bulbs are in flower, with little or no interruption in the vegetative process.

Once an eye has begun to swell, water should be supplied and it should be encouraged to grow at maximum capacity because future development and flowers depend upon it.

The frequency of watering depends upon the climate, the amount of sunlight, the temperature, the daylength, and most of all upon the potting medium.

If you remember that in the natural habitats cattleya roots are partially exposed to air, if not entirely, you will not soak the medium consistently to the exclusion of air. OVERWATERING IS THE GREATEST FAULT OF ALL NOVICE GROWERS.

There are so many different potting mixes that a positive guide rule is impossible. Potting mixes are described in the chapter on Potting.

Cattleyas in nature are not constantly wet at the roots, but often soaked and quickly dried out.

When you do water, do it thoroughly. Pour water into the pot with a water breaker nozzle or a mist nozzle so you apply water in quantity to soak all the pot without washing the medium out of the container. Let the water run out of the bottom of the pot and soak it again. The reason for this is to leach out the fertilizer salts which, if allowed to accumulate, may burn the roots.

Seedlings and small mericlones need frequent watering. The smaller the pots the faster they dry out. Specimen plants in very large pots need to be grown in a porous medium or the roots in the center will rot because the material will never dry thoroughly.

In cold weather when the night is cooler than the day, water in the

Epidendrums

Epidendrum teretifolia flowers are
dark green

Epidendrum coronatum
(E. moyobambae)

Epidendrum exasperatum grows five feet tall

morning so plants are partially dry by night. And take care in cool weather that water does not stand in the partially folded mature leaves as it may cause rot. Bifoliates hold their developing leaves upward and catch water like a funnel. Unifoliate cattleyas may have the top of the eighth sarong leaf protruding above the point where the true leaf and bulb join and catch water in the crevice. Make a small slit in the still-green sarong to let water escape.

When orchids are grown as houseplants it is not possible to water them with a watering can or pitcher where they sit upon a table or window-sill. The only way is to carry the pots to the sink or basin or bathtub and let water run through and repeat, leaving them to drain.

This also applies to orchids under lights on tiered carts as watering needs to be thorough, and if it is there will be run off.

Watering is allied to the intensity of the light, the temperature, air movement, humidity and all other factors of the environment.

Temperature of the water is not important except that it should be approximately air temperature in winter, not icy, certainly, and not hot in summer. If you use a garden hose for watering and it lies out in the summer sun, the water inside should be run off before applying to plants as it is likely to be boiling hot.

Orchids tolerate a wide range of water types, and generally what comes through the pipes is suitable. If all the plants in a collection are ailing, it would pay to have the water content analyzed.

HUMIDITY — Humidity is the moisture of the atmosphere. It is important to orchids.

High humidity slows down the escape of water vapor into the air from the leaves. Laundry on a line dries faster when the air is dry than when it is humid. Dry air pulls moisture out of plants at a rapid rate.

Therefore, the water vapor given off in respiration, which goes on night and day, is not transpired so readily when the air is humid.

The atmosphere need not be sopping, but moist air is desirable. In dry climates, evaporative coolers can achieve a desirable atmosphere. In more humid areas where only occasional midday humidifying is needed, a system of mist nozzles mounted on copper tubing along the rafters which connects with the hose can fill the air with moisture in a few minutes.

Any humidity device should break the water up into minute droplets of fine mist that are not heavy enough to carry fungus spores. Do not mist foliage in chilly weather or just before a temperature drop.

Use mist to lower leaf temperature so that high light intensity and heat can be endured. Evaporating water helps to absorb the heat.

Humidifiers are useful in climates where the air is dry and temperature is high, and the extended use of artificial heat dries out the atmosphere.

The lack of humidity in our homes is one reason growing orchids indoors is difficult. If light and temperature conditions are acceptable, probably the bathroom or kitchen are the best locations for orchids because of the moisture in the air.

Fertilizer

Time was when orchids were grown in osmunda and nobody used fertilizer. Now many mediums are in use, and everybody adds fertilizer, even to osmunda.

There is a bewildering array of orchid fertilizers available. For you who are just starting with orchids, the best way is to consult the grower from whom you buy your plants and continue with whatever fertilizer and schedule he has been giving them. But by the time you acquire plants from several sources in several different mediums this is not practical and you must put them all in whatever medium and on whatever fertilizer works best under your conditions.

Plants growing in bark require a higher nitrogen formula and more of it than plants in other mediums because the fungus that destroys the wood feeds on nitrogen, and if it is not in the fertilizer it is stolen from the plants.

However, overfertilizing in any compost causes roots to rot and plants can't live without functioning roots.

The timing and type of fertilizer depends upon the potting material and the growth cycle. Plants are never at a complete standstill, as we know that photosynthesis and respiration go on all the time to repair

Schombocattleya Trudy Fennell (Cattleya
granulosa x Schomburgkia thomsoniana)

Cattleytonia Rosy Jewel 'Orchidglade' A.M./AOS
(Cattleya bowringiana x Broughtonia sanguinea)

and maintain tissues. However, when there is no visible growth, less fertilizer is needed and the quantity and frequency should be cut down.

The major numbers on a fertilizer package stand for the percentages of nitrogen, phosphorus and potassium in that order. Nitrogen is essential to growth; phosphorus aids in production of new tissues, flowers and seeds. Potassium helps to mature growth.

Therefore, a balanced 10-10-10 or similar number is a good choice for all potting materials and all seasons except for plants grown in bark. Bark-grown plants must have a 30-10-10 formula.

Too much fertilizer is harmful, so it is important to mix whatever brand you buy at exactly the specified rate, and to apply only at the frequency recommended.

Trace elements are minor elements needed by all plants and are included in minute proportions in almost all packaged fertilizers. Read the fine print on the label to be sure.

An important factor in fertilizing is that of leaching out the fertilizer by applying clear water every so often. Fertilizer salts tends to accumulate, and when the concentration is too strong where roots touch them, roots will be damaged. Leaching particularly applies to bark growers who often run dilute solutions of fertilizer in with regular waterings.

Remember the ratio of light, heat and humidity to the rate of photosynthesis and adjust your fertilizer schedule accordingly. When there are dull days, heavy smog or low temperatures the photosynthetic rate is slowed down and the fertilizer rate should be, too.

The reverse is true when temperature is high and light is bright. You will increase watering and you can increase fertilizer. Do not make heavier doses, but give lighter applications more often. Plants grown outdoors in warm weather need fertilizer adjusted according to the amount of rainfall.

FOLIAR FEEDING — Recent research at the University of Florida demonstrated that orchid plants can absorb nutrients through their leaves. Radioactive materials traced the nutrients both forward and backward through the plants. Applied to the leaves, in 10 hours 54 percent of the material was located in the pseudobulbs, and in 12 hours 11 percent was found in the roots.

Foliar feeding is easy to do with a soluble fertilizer and a hose jar attachment that siphons it out. It should not replace root feeding, and the total amount of fertilizer used in a month (or other given period) by root and leaf application should not exceed the total amount recommended for that brand.

It is easy to dissolve the fertilizer in a small amount of warm water before mixing it in quantity.

There are slow-release fertilizers in pellet form that are available. Follow directions carefully especially as to giving sufficient water at intervals to release the nutrients.

Extra fertilizer is no cure for poor environment or neglect. It must be related to the growth factors to be useful and effective.

Cattleya Jose Marti (C. Bob Betts x C. Bow Bells)

CHAPTER III

THE FLOWERS

The purpose of any flower is to attract an insect that will bring pollen for fertilization so seeds are produced and the species is maintained.

The orchid flower is wonderously constructed to do just that. And Nature is so intricately balanced in all details that there live in the same area pollinators (insects or birds) that are attracted to and equipped to transfer pollen from one flower to another of the same or comparable type.

The outstanding characteristic of the orchid flower is the lip or labellum, which often serves as a landing strip for a flying bee. The lip may be brightly marked with yellow eyes like spotlights on either side of the column where the pollen is located, or with lines leading to this point. Or even with raised bumps or hairs to assist him in walking the right direction after he lands and folds his wings. Furthermore, the nectar which he seeks is so located that the insect must brush against the pollen to reach it. Sometimes the flower even rubs a sticky substance on his back first so the pollen will adhere. It is all very ingenious.

The flowers of the Cattleya group are divided into six easily identified segments. (See sketches of representative flowers.) All orchids have these parts, but in some flowers they are fused, modified or not otherwise so distinct.

Examine an open cattleya flower. It has three narrow segments that are the outside ones when it is still a bud and so are attached lowest on the stem (pedicel) at the back of the flower. These are the sepals. One sepal stands up at the top of the flower, the other two spread to form the points of a triangle. They are the same color as the two large horizontal petals.

The sepals on a rose, for instance, are the little green pointed bits which enclose the bud when it is very small. They do not change color nor grow in size as the flower matures, and on an open rose the sepals can be seen at the bottom of the flower, still small, pointed and green.

The other three segments of the orchid flower are petals. There are two identical wing-like petals, and the lip which is a petal but which is different from the other two.

The lip is usually more brightly colored than the sepals and petals, or different in color and pattern. The lip may be ruffled or fringed.

When the flower is a bud, all of these three petals are folded up inside the sepals and the lip is pointing upward. As the flower gets ready to open, the flower stem twists itself 90 degrees so that when it opens the lip is outward and almost flat and suitable for a landing platform. The twisting process is called resupination and is peculiar to orchids.

A flower worn as a corsage or used in an arrangement should be placed as it grows, not head down nor lip up. Remember the bee.

Sepals and petals collectively are sometimes called tepals.

The lip is more or less tubular at the top and encloses within the tube a club-shaped organ called the column. This contains the reproductive parts, both male and female. It is usually white and waxy.

On a lily, for example, there are separate anthers topped with pollen grains, and a central stigma leading to the ovary for receiving the pollen. Everything is rolled into one in the orchid column.

◀ **Center flower: Cattleya hybrid. Others clockwise from top right: Cattleya amethystoglossa, Laelia purpurata, Brassavola digbyana, Laelia cinnabarina, Sophronitis coccinea, Epidendrum atropurpureum.**

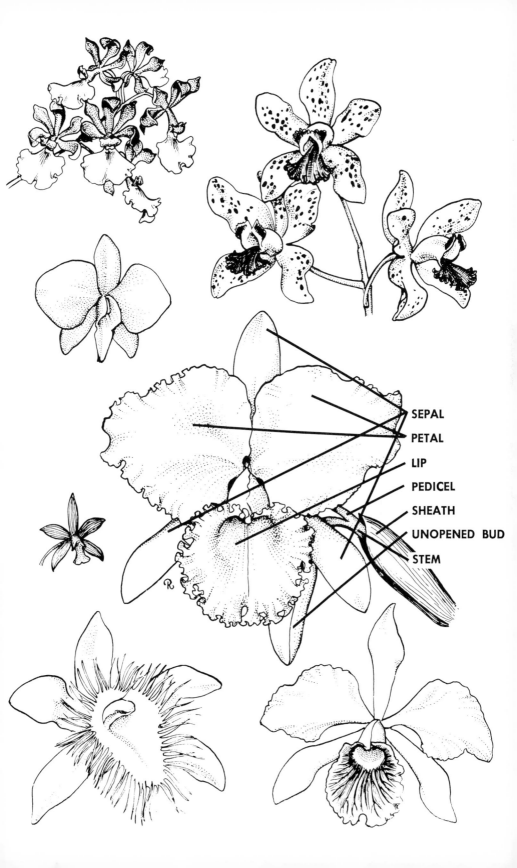

SEPAL

PETAL

LIP

PEDICEL

SHEATH

UNOPENED BUD

STEM

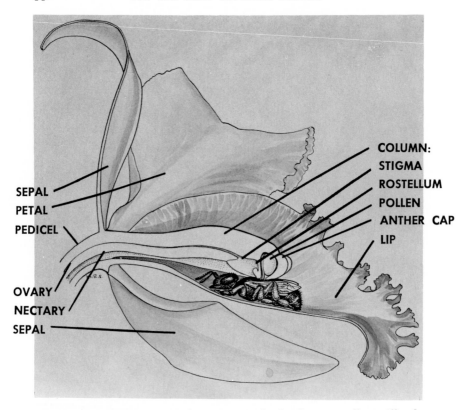

SEPAL
PETAL
PEDICEL

COLUMN:
STIGMA
ROSTELLUM
POLLEN
ANTHER CAP
LIP

OVARY
NECTARY
SEPAL

Bee entering flower to reach nectar. As he backs out pollen will adhere to his back.

Follow the sketch and view the column from the side. From front to back it is basically like this.

The cap on the forward end is the anther cap which may be knocked off by an insect or a tool in the process of pollination. This is part of the pollen bearing structure along with the stamen and filament.

The pollen grains, which in cattleyas are visibly hard, waxy pinheads, are attached back of the anther cap on the underside of the column. Everything is on the underside, since the bee lights on the lip and crawls beneath the column to reach the nectary.

Next there is a partition between the pollen and the cavity behind it. This partition is called the rostellum and it has two functions. One, it prevents self-pollination of the flower by separating the pollen and stigma, and two, it rubs glue on the back of the bee so the pollen sticks as he flies away with it.

The cavity that comes next is the stigma, where pollen grains are deposited. It contains a sticky solution to hold them. They germinate in this solution then grow down the column into the ovules which are located in the ovary in what looks from the outside like the green stem of the flower. If seed forms, it is this upper stem (pedicel) that swells and becomes the seed pod. The colorful flower parts that served their purpose in bringing the bee, wither and turn brown at the end. After a flower has been pollinated it folds up. Its mission is accomplished.

The nectary, the bee's destination, is a tube embedded in the base of the flower in the cattleya group.

So the bee crawls under the cattleya column to reach the nectar. As he backs out, if he had pollen on his back, it would adhere to the sticky liquid in the stigmatic cavity. Next he passes the rostellum which smears glue on his thorax, and as he passes beneath the pollen grains, they stick to the glue. Then away he goes—to another flower and deposits the pollen in the stigma as he backs out of that bloom. And he dislodges the pollen from that flower and carries it to the next one.

All of this is basic for cattleyas which are bee-pollinated flowers. Other insects are pollinators for other flowers in this group but the system is similar in pattern.

Orchids do smell. Anybody who thinks they do not has not been in a greenhouse. Some are fragrant during the day during the hours their pollinators are moving about. Others, like Brassavola nodosa, are fragrant at night because they are trying to attract night-flying pollinators. It is all part of the allure.

Time of Bloom

Going back to the species, each has a definite time of bloom which is partially explained in Chapter I.

With hybrids many generations advanced from the species, and descended from several species, the blooming periods get more varied but may fall into general seasonal categories.

In my greenhouse the same plants bloom in the same months year after year, but not every plant of the same hybrid blooms at exactly the same time. This is true with mericlones, for with many plants of a single propagation the flowering season spreads over several weeks.

Daylength and temperature are factors which affect flower development, which is the crucial point in blooming. Some commercial crops are timed to bloom for holidays by lengthening or shortening the days of light-controllable plants.

Short-day plants are those which normally begin development of the buds when the nights are long ($12\frac{1}{2}$ to $13\frac{1}{2}$ hours). To induce them to bloom earlier, black cloth around them cuts off all the light for a certain number of hours to make for a longer period of darkness.

In reverse, to prevent short-day plants from developing buds when the days are naturally short, lights are turned on for two or three hours in the middle of the night to break the long hours of darkness, and these plants do not develop buds until the lights are omitted and the nights are long.

It is not worthwhile trying to do this in a small amateur collection, but for commercial growers, hitting the holidays with blooms is important.

Flower initiation and flower development are two different processes. Flower buds are initiated in the meristem, which is the growing point in the new lead, when the lead is less than one inch long. This is a process whereby plant tissue becomes specialized into that which can become flowers rather than leaves or other plant parts.

Flower development is triggered by environmental factors at some time when the new bulb is mature or almost mature. In fact, it is probable that environmental factors, notably daylight, temperature and possibly daylength, are vital to both these processes at some precise times in development of the new bulb, but we know very little about this yet. But remember that the food manufactured in the plant is used first for survival, then for growth, then for flowers, so if flowers are to initiate and to develop (which may be several months later), the conditions and care of the plant must be better than adequate.

In building up an amateur collection you want to balance your blooming times so you will have flowers at all seasons, not all at one time of year. Make your purchases with this thought in mind, but be prepared for flexibility as some hybrids bloom three times in two years, some twice a year, and some vary with the weather if you have a cool spring, early fall, or a long period of cloudy days.

Good Qualities of Flowers

You don't need to be a judge to judge your own flowers. Not all the blooms in your collection, in fact none of them, need to be prize-winners. Indeed some of the best orchids never get shown. But still, you might as well have quality flowers. Be guided by your own tastes. Plants don't have to be awarded to be good, but if you buy seedlings of proven or awarded parents, mericlones of quality flowers, and flowers you like, you can't go too far wrong.

However, you can be guided by the points the judges consider when you make your choice of a plant in bloom. If your growing space is overcrowded and some plants have to go, consider your preference and the quality of the flowers.

Personal preference can't be measured by anybody else. If you like a flower enough to give the plant room and take care of it, then it matters not what it might win in competition in an orchid show. But when you are adding plants you might as well get good ones in your taste range, and they need not necessarily be high in price.

Here are the points on the American Orchid Society judging scale for Cattleyas and related flowers.

Form, 30 points: The ideal form of a Cattleya is a round flower, well balanced, with the sepals and petals in proportion to each other and placed evenly. In advanced unifoliate hybrids the petals should overlap the sepals so there are no spaces in between. In other types you need to know the parentage and background to judge if the form is good for the type that it is. Some Laelia and Brassavola species tend to breed narrow sepals, but this is to be expected.

Don't buy cripples that are distorted in any segments or in the color, but don't throw out a plant that blooms crippled once as it may not do so again. Do not judge seedlings on the first blooming as they may be better the second time if you grow them well.

Color, also 30 points: Color varies from pure white to very dark but not black. Some flowers have spots, stripes, or other markings. Whatever the color is it should be clear and alive, not streaked or faltering at the edges. No dirty white, dull yellow or muddy purple. Lightness or darkness is a personal choice, but whatever the color it should be pleasing, and if there are two or more colors in the flower, they should be harmonious or effective in contrast.

Size, only 10 points: Size depends a lot on both inheritance and on how well you grew the plant. You might buy a mericlone or a selfed seedling advertised as having seven-inch blooms, but if you fail to grow the plant well, it may have only four inch blooms, if any. The biggest flowers are not necessarily the best and many of the smaller types have great charm.

Substance and texture, 20 points: Substance has to do with the thickness of the flower, whether it is flimsy like nylon or heavy like oilcloth. Some of the bifoliate cattleyas are very waxy and stiff, some of the big cattleyas are quite delicate. All should hold their petals and sepals erect and not be floppy. Texture is a surface quality and orchids often look like they are brushed with stardust. The surface should be glistening and alive, not dull.

Floriferousness and stem, 10 points: Floriferousness depends upon heredity more than culture, but good culture can produce a maximum number of flowers on each lead. Some hybrids never have more than two flowers to a stem, others can be depended upon for three or four. The stem, part of the point score, should be sufficiently sturdy to hold the blooms above the foliage, and flowers should space themselves so they do not crowd each other.

You can study these flower qualities in the blue ribbon winners at orchid shows, in photographs in the commercial nursery catalogs, or in the awards records of the American Orchid Society.

American Orchid Society awards, given for flower quality are indicated as follows:

F.C.C. means First Class Certificate, indicates average of scoring by three judges at 90 points or more.

A.M. means Award of Merit, 80 to 89 points.

H.C.C. means High Class Certificate, 75-79 points.

A plant which has been awarded carries the award in these abbreviations after its name followed by AOS, RHS, or other initials to indicate the organization that granted the award, American Orchid Society, Royal Horticultural Society, and other national and regional organizations. Some organizations give awards with different titles, and the AOS has a number of awards in addition to the above. These refer to permanent awards, not to temporary show awards.

Divisions of awarded plants carry the award, but not its seedlings. However, many catalogs list seedlings by giving the names and awards of the parents so your chances of getting good quality are reasonable.

Mericlones of awarded plants are offered in great profusion. Mericlones are cheaper than bulb divisions of awarded plants, but about equal in price with seedlings of comparable size which offer an element of surprise.

**Epicattleya Rosita 'Richard Roth'
A.M./AOS**

Laeliacattleya Eva, small orange flowers.

CHAPTER IV

HEREDITY
AND HYBRIDS

The "Cattleya Alliance" is not a political organization, but a broad term for the plants of genera related to Cattleyas, and the hybrids of this group.

Orchids are like dogs except in these flowers the mixing of breeds is purposeful and some of the finest flowers are truly mongrels as far as mixed parentage goes. Those of mixed (but recorded) ancestry may have the best qualities of the breeding lines involved.

Well known hybrids are the laeliocattleyas, usually with the size of the cattleya ancestry and intensified color due to the laelia influence. Or the brassolaeliocattleyas which add fringe to the lip from Brassavola digbyana.

There are many more combinations, and the conglomerates are as diverse in their make-up as conglomerates on the stock market. For a list of multi-generic hybrids and their components see page 138.

Like the Colonial Dames of America, the orchid hybrids can trace their ancestry step by step, and all the way to the species besides. So this is where we begin.

The genus Cattleya is composed of about 50 species divided into the two groups discussed in Chapter I—unifoliate or labiate (meaning big lip) and bifoliate or cluster types which have smaller but often more numerous flowers.

Space neither permits nor requires an enumeration of the species. Present day hybrids are several generations removed, but you can see the influence of the ancestors. I suggest that as you visit orchid shows and nurseries you observe the species on display and note their characteristics. See the book list, too.

The first cattleya arrived in England in 1818. Mr. William Cattley had imported some lichens from Brazil and the shipment arrived with peculiar, unknown plants tied around the lichens as protective wrapping. Mr. Cattley had enough curiosity to save the unknown plants and was able to keep them alive and bloom them. Imagine the sensation when they produced big purple blooms in 1823 or 1824.

PURPLE CATTLEYAS — The first plant was called Cattleya labiata. The genus name honors Mr. Cattley and the species name indicates, the prominent lip.

Many other species were sent to England as collectors began searching for them in the American tropics. A number of these species are now recognized by taxonomists as varieties of Cattleya labiata, but we amateur growers write and speak about them as if they were distinct species. For instance, the botanists write Cattleya labiata var. mossiae, but we say Cattleya mossiae.

Cattleya mossiae is one that you will meet often either in species form or in its progeny. For many years millions of mossiaes were grown for Easter corsages, but now they have largely been replaced by their hybrids which have improved form and substance and have lost a lot of the floppiness of the species.

The same goes for Cattleya trianaei, which was the Christmas orchid until its descendants took over.

The large purples, for the most part, go back to the labiata group: Cattleya gaskelliana, C. warscewiczii (also called C. gigas), C. percivaliana, C. lueddemanniana (also called C. speciosissima), C. mendellii and others. (Note: C. is the abbreviation for Cattleya when followed by a species or hybrid name but not when the word is alone.)

Some of the important primary (first generation) hybrids that are ancestors of many modern hybrids include: C. Enid (C. mossiae X C. warscewiczii, registered first in 1898 but remade many times and used for parentage many times) ; C. Ballantineana (C. trianaei X C. warcewiczii, 1889) ; C. hardyana (C. dowiana X C. warscewiczii, natural hybrid remade by man); and C. Maggie Raphael (C. dowiana x C. trianaei, 1889).

You can use the hybrid lists (see book list) and trace your plants back through each generation, making a family tree with horizontal and vertical lines. You will find that many hybrids are now so complex that they go back to several species, or to one species several times.

WHITE CATTLEYAS — The large white cattleyas are derived from the white (alba) forms of the labiata group.

Cattleya Bow Bells, registered by Black & Flory Ltd. of England in 1945 brought white cattleyas to superlative quality only a few generations removed from the species. The name honors St. Mary-le-Bow Church in the old City of London. Anyone who was born and raised within the sound of the Bow bells is a cockney.

Bow Bells, the flower, is a cross of C. Edithiae X C. Suzanne Hye. C. Suzanne Hye, registered by Jules Hye of Ghent in 1906, is C. gaskelliana alba X C. mossiae 'Wageneri', this last usually called "mossiae wag." The other parent, C. Edithiae, is C. trianaei alba and C. Suzanne Hye again.

Then there is C. Joyce Hannington, registered by Ernest Dane of Massachusetts, also in 1945. This one goes back to alba forms of C. labiata twice, C. schroderae, C. trianaei, C. lueddemanniana, C. gaskelliana, and C. mossiae 'Wageneri.'

C. Edithiae has produced many fine progeny, and from Bow Bells has come such hybrids as C. Bob Betts (X C. mossiae 'Wageneri'), C. General Patton (X C. Barbara Billingsley), and C. Madeleine Knowlton (X. C. Joyce Hannington).

Of course there are other notable white hybrids, among them C. Barbara Billingsley, descended from C. trianaei 'Broomhills'; and C. White Empress ("mossiae wag" twice, trianaei and gaskelliana.) And there are more good whites appearing all the time.

You can't tell by the hybrid lists which are the white forms if the species has both purple and alba types. The older lists sometimes indicated the varieties used but the newer compilations do not as any two parents produce progeny with the designated name once the cross is registered. Thus the cross of a purple C. gaskelliana and purple C. mossiae would still make C. Suzanne Hye, but purple.

However, when you buy seedlings, the parentage should include varietal or cultivar names, if any, along with awards of parents, if any.

SEMI-ALBAS — Large cattleyas of the semi-alba type (also called white-with-colored-lip) are likewise derived from variations of the species. C. mossiae 'Reineckiana', for example, is a large flower with the typical C. mossiae shape, white petals and sepals and a lip marked with lavender. Its value lies in size, spring-flowering, and vigor. It is a fine parent.

Cattleya warscewiczii 'Frau Melanie Beyrodt' is abbreviated 'F.M.B.' (and usually called "gigas F.M.B.") has an almost solid purple lip, the size and shape of C. warscewiczii (C. gigas), but rather poor substance. Alba forms of C. labiata, C. trianaei and others have been used in breeding. Some good flowers are turning up as tetraploid parents become available, and while the award-winning semi-albas are fewer in number than the lavenders or whites, the percentage should increase with newer hybrids.

SPLASHED PETAL CATTLEYAS — Cattleyas with spalshed petals are a small group, but some are very startling flowers which look like they have three lips and three sepals. They trace back to C. intermedia var. aquinii, an unusual form of a normally white cattleya that was found in Brazil prior to 1900. By crossing this with other flowers with some veining on the petals, or with this type of marking in their ancestry, notably C. mendelii, C. trianaei 'Gratrixiae', additional splash petals have been obtained. C. intermedia var. aquinii has been selfed, so plants are available. C. Suavior 'Aquinii' has been meristemmed, and there are a number of splash-petal seedlings coming along. Flowers in this group are novelties but their bizarre markings add interest to a collection.

YELLOWS — Yellow cattleyas and those called art shades very often go back to C. dowiana var. aurea. The list of hybrids from this species is lengthy, as is the list from some of its primary hybrids such as C. Fabia (C. dowiana X C. labiata.) Many of these crosses were made with the hope of getting improved yellow flowers, but even when the flower is purple, the yellow in the background usually enhances the color.

For many years the yellows were often disappointing. Many of them with C. bicolor in the parentage tend to have spade lips, knotty or crippled petals, and were difficult to grow. Now, however, hybridizing is so many generations advanced that fine yellows in large and small sizes are available. And when you come to one like Blc. Malworth you will find in its background that C. dowiana appears eight times, C. bicolor twice, Laelia xanthina twice and L. cinnabarina once plus other species. In Lc. Mem. Albert Heinecke, which has butter yellow sepals and petals and a wine red lip, C. dowiana appears 11 times in its ancestry, C. bicolor four times and Laelia tenebrosa twice.

Laelias have been used, too, in the search for gold. More and more small cluster hybrids are appearing with Laelia flava, L. cinnabarina and L. tenebrosa in the background. Sophronitis species, C. bicolor and C. aurantiaca are used as parents, too.

In the series of Lc. Orange Ann, Lc. Orange Beauty, and Lc. Orange Gem you will find the colors come from Laelia cinnabarina and L. harpophylla.

When, in turn, the small yellows are crossed with large purple or white cattleya hybrids, size and shape are often improved and fine big yellow flowers result.

Surprisingly, some of the good semi-albas have C. dowiana var. aurea in their background, for when crossed with a pure white cattleya the yellow sepals and petals are dominated by the white, but the brightly colored lip carries over to the offspring.

RED CATTLEYAS — Red cattleyas are becoming more plentiful with the use of green pod culture for getting viable seeds, and by use of selected parents that breed good color. There is a lot we don't understand about color pigments and their behavior, and there is sometimes considerable variation within the flock of seedlings, but more and more good reddish-purple, reddish-orange and reddish-bronze flowers are being seen. Quite red are certain flowers of Lc. Marie Ozella, Slc. Paprika, Slc, Jewel Box, C. Nigrella, Lc. Lee Langford and Potinara Gordon Siu.

Some people see the two-inch orange-red flowers of Laelia milleri as a route to red, already showing up in such hybrids as Lc. Rojo, Lc. Orangeham and Lc. Desert Orange.

Actually, if red is hard to achieve in big cattleya type flowers it may be because nature is opposed to it. Cal Dodson in discussing pollination of orchid flowers (see book list) tells us that some bees are blind to red, and since cattleyas are bee-pollinated flowers, you can see why nature would not want them to be red. They would not attract the insects to perpetuate them. Nature reckons without man, who is busier than any bee pollinating orchids by hand, but neither does she depend on him.

Brassavola digbyana contributes fringe to the lip.

Epidendrum mariae is a parent of some green orchids.

GREEN FLOWERS — Green orchids in this group are something else again. Cattleya granulosa, the sensational Cattleya guttata alba, Epidendrum mariae, Epidendrum tampense alba and Brassavola nodosa are among the parents of the greens.

Some of their offspring are as green as grass. Usually the seedlings of a flock vary from greenish-yellow into yellow and green. Epidendrum Memoria Young C. Lott (E. tampense alba X E. mariae) is white and very green and is charming.

BLUE CATTLEYAS — The so-called blues in the cattleya group are those which tend towards violet-blue or lilac rather than reddish-purple. The blues are scarce but breeding continues. Blue strains of Cattleya bowringiana, C. trianaei, C. intermedia, C. amethystoglossa and others offer possibilities for developing blue flowers with better shape and color in future generations.

Bifoliate Cattleyas

The bifoliate or cluster cattleyas are attractive and are gaining in popularity because of their curious flowers, unusual colors, and manageable flower size. Not everybody can wear a seven-inch purple orchid. The smaller flowers are suitable for many occasions for corsages, useful in arrangements and decorative in the greenhouse or on the windowsill. Amateur growers like variety.

Some of the bifoliate flowers are waxy and long lasting, while others may be short lived.

Cattleya guttata is a great favorite for breeding unusual cattleya hybrids. It has very heavy, waxy flowers of green or bronze with reddish spots and white and amethyst lips in clusters atop tall slender bulbs. C. guttata var. leopoldii has smaller but more numerous flowers, brown or green spotted with purple. The hybrids of these two, made with several genera including Cattleya, Epidendrum, Laeliocattleya, Potinara, Epigoa, and Schomburgkia, have produced fascinating flowers.

Cattleya bicolor, C. granulosa, and C. forbesii are contributing to the art shade hybrids, and C. amethystoglossa's jewel tones are showing up in its progeny.

Cattleya bowringiana and C. skinneri are familiar species with small lavender flowers, and C. bowringiana has been used to make hybrids of good form and medium size.

C. intermedia and C. loddigesii are similar with four-inch flowers of lilac and heavy substance. The white forms of both species are good parents. The famous white bifoliate, C. loddigesii 'Stanley's' has been crossed with large unifoliate whites to make such beauties as C. Henrietta Japhet, C. Eileen Wilson and C. Margaret Stewart. (Cattleya harrisoniae and C. harrisoniana, mentioned frequently in orchid literature, have been identified as C. loddigesii.)

Laelias

The genus Laelia has thirty species, more or less, generally of smaller flowers and plants than the cattleyas but often with brilliant color: yellow, orange, red and magenta.

Laelias are not grouped according to one or two leaves, but more by the shape of the pseudobulbs which may be round, flat and wrinkled like turtles, or tall and thin.

Laelia flowers are, as a rule, smaller and more open than cattleyas because their sepals and petals are narrower. They frequently have a starry shape. As in cattleyas, the sepals and two petals are of similar color, the lip usually more brilliant and with additional colors. The laelia lip has three distinct lobes, as do some cattleya lips, with the two side lobes often forming the long narrow tube around the column.

Laelia anceps, L. flava and others are often grown in amateur collections for their charming flowers.

A great many of the large flowered cattleya hybrids are actually bigeneric hybrids between Cattleya and Laelia named Laeliocattleya. The abbreviation is Lc.

The large Laelia purpurata is in the ancestry of a vast number of hybrids. This species is native to the coast of Brazil from Sao Paulo to Porto Alegre. It varies in color from pure white, white petals and sepals with purple lips to lavender petals and sepals with dark purple lips. There are many varieties.

Figuring importantly in the hybrid lists, and the plants in your collection, are plants with Laelia purpurata parentage. Lc. Canhamiana, a primary hybrid first made by Veitch in 1885 by crossing C. mossiae X Laelia purpurata, is important in hybridizing in both lavenders and semialbas. The comparatively narrow sepals of the purpuratas are improved by breeding with cattleyas, and the color of the cattleyas is enhanced by that of the laelias.

Brassavolas

Brassavolas are important in hybridizing, especially Brassavola digbyana. This is a greenish white flower with an enormous deeply fringed lip which adds size and edging when bred with cattleyas and laeliocattleyas. Brassocattleyas and brassolaeliocattleyas, abbreviated Bc. and Blc. are popular in orchid collections.

Brassavola glauca, a small waxy flower, has been used a bit for hybridizing, and Brassavola nodosa is a popular parent for novelty crosses. It has very thin green sepals and petals and a white heart-shaped lip. The foliage is like green pencils.

B. digbyana and B. glauca have been botanically reclassified into the genus Rhyncholaelia, but you need not worry about this as Brassavola is retained for their horticultural name and that is what we call them.

There are a dozen or more species of Brassavola coming from the West Indies and parts of South America. They grow well with cattleyas but like brighter sun if possible. Brassavola nodosa is called "lady-of-the-night" because of its nocturnal fragrance. It grows on rocks by the sea in Panama but adapts to pot or slab culture. Grow at least one plant to put in your outdoor barbecue area when it blooms.

Sophronitis

Brilliant color is achieved from Sophronitis coccinea (synonym S. grandiflora.) It has small flowers on small plants which are inclined to be temperamental to grow. The blooms are bright orange or red, and sometimes impart their color when bred with bigger blooms.

Sophrolaeliocattleyas are increasing in number and should be observed at shows and nurseries. The most famous one is Slc. Anzac, which has been used many times as a parent.

The other five Sophronitis species aside from S. coccinea are curiosities.

Epidendrums

Epidendrums should be a whole book, and maybe they will be if I live long enough. There are thousands of species, nobody knows exactly how many. Most of them grow in the American tropics and sub-tropics. Several are indigenous in Florida. E. conopseum is the hardiest of the lot and can be found northward onto the coast of North Carolina.

Epidendrums are divided into several groups. Most easily distinguished are the reed-stems because the plants have tall slender stems like bamboo but not rigid, no pseudobulbs, and many leaves along both sides. They produce long flower stems from the tops of the canes bearing clusters of tiny flowers in perfect shapes and jewel colors.

The reed-stem epis are delightful for garden orchids in warm climates, and for boutonnieres anywhere. They are almost everblooming if given enough sun.

Laelia purpurata
alba

Epidendrum ibaguense, commonly called E. radicans, is the one that is commonly grown in all its color variations. The plants make keikis easily and soon become columnar jumbles of stems, roots, leaves and flowers.

The encyclias have distinct pseudobulbs, some round like eggs, some taller and thinner, with leaves at the top and flowers on stems from the top of the bulbs. Some taxonomists say the encyclias should be a separate genus because most of them are pollinated by bees and the other epidendrums by moths, butterflies or birds.

Epidendrum atropurpureum is a favorite in this section. The pseudobulbs are like green hen's eggs, the leaves long and strap-shaped. The flowers have mouse colored or chocolate curved sepals and petals, and broad white or pink lips each with one magenta blotch.

E. ciliare, C. cochleatum, and the common Florida E. tampense are worth growing. Some interesting hybrids—Epicattleyas, Epilaelias, and Epilaeliocattleyas—are among the multigenerics that might interest you.

Schomburgkias

These are generally large plants, similar to the laelias in character. The pseudobulbs range from 9 inches to 24 inches high, topped with narrow leathery leaves and flower scapes often four feet tall. For all this effort, the flowers tend to have narrow segments that are often wavy.

Hybridizing with cattleyas and other genera has tended to improve the form of the flowers and sometimes to reduce the size of the plants to dimensions more manageable in small greenhouses.

Additional Genera

There are other genera that are closely related to the cattleyas and grown with them and hybridized with them and with each other. Among the ones we hear about are Barkeria, Broughtonia, Diacrium, Laeliopsis, and Cattleyopsis. Make their acquaintance when you have an opportunity.

Cattleya Enid alba

CHAPTER V

ORCHID NAMES

You have been reading all these names and becoming familiar with them. Now let us see how orchids get their names.

The plant family containing all the orchids is the Orchidaceae. It is enormous and believed to include ten percent of all the flowering plants in the world.

In the family there are subfamilies, tribes and subtribes, which need not concern you since these are matters for botanists and taxonomists. We are dealing with a subtribe named Laelieae or Epidendrinae, depending upon which classification system you follow.

Then comes the genus. There are probably 600 genera in the orchid family. Genera is plural of genus. A genus is a group of plants with similar characteristics that warrant lumping them together.

Basically plant names follow a binomial system. The genus name comes first and is capitalized (and sometimes italicized) and is like the last name of a person but like a Chinaman. The last name comes first. Hence Cattleya is a genus name.

The rose family, Rosaceae, contains only about 100 genera. Besides roses (Rosa), there are Pyracantha, Cotoneaster, Pyrus (pears), and Malus (apples).

Next comes the species name, called the specific epithet, indicating a particular kind of plant within this genus in its original form. Take

Cattleya mossiae. Cattleya is the genus name and mossiae is the species name. The two names are written or spoken in that order, group name first. Just like our names in the telephone book but without the commas: Smith, Henry; Smith, John; Smith, Walter. So: Cattleya gaskelliana, Cattleya warneri, Cattleya elongata. Generic names are usually abbreviated, C. for Cattleya, when a species or hybrid name follows if it has been spelled out previously.

The species name is written in small letters, is in italics if the genus name is in italics.

A third term may be added if certain wild plants have certain characteristics different from the usual run of that species. The abbreviation var. and a Latin term to describe the distinctive feature follow and become the varietal name. Var. is the abbreviation for variety.

Neither the abbreviation var. nor the name is capitalized, but the name may be in italics if previous names are. Cattleya dowiana indicates the form of the species having petals flecked with crimson. Cattleya dowiana var. aurea indicates that it has clear yellow sepals and petals.

A third or fourth term is called a cultivar epithet, which applies to any cultivated individual plant of a hybrid or species or to a botanical variety whether collected in the wild or raised in cultivation. This term is not in italics, is enclosed within single quotes (not double quotes), and begins with a capital letter. It does not have the abbreviation var. before it although this may appear earlier in the sequence if the plant is a botanical variety. Examples: Cattleya walkeriana alba 'Orchidglade', and Cattleya granulosa 'Tracy Lynn.'

(Editor's note: We have not used italic print in this book because of production costs and easier reading when all is in Roman type.)

You will acquire some plants labeled with cultivar epithets, and every division, back bulb or mericlone of any plant so named carries the same cultivar epithet. You may name any of your plants that are not already so labeled, but this is not customary unless they are awarded or they have some outstanding horticultural quality.

To keep your records straight, you can use numbers if you have more than one plant of a species or a hybrid, such as Cattleya rex #1 and Cattleya rex #2. Then if you divide either one of them, retain the number on the division and use letters to indicate individuals such as C. rex #1-A.

Lc. Areca 'Model' F.C.C./AOS was awarded in 1957.

Natural hybrids, those hybrids made between two species by insects the first time (but possibly repeated by man later) are named in Latin like the species and printed in italics and small letters just like the specific epithet or species name. Example: Cattleya hardyana, natural hybrid of C. dowiana X C. warscewiczii.

Man-made hybrids, which are what we grow the most, have the same formula for naming but with adaptations.

The generic name is the first term, and it may be a single genus or a multigeneric compound name. Examples: Cattleya Cleasiana, a hybrid of C. intermedia X C. loddigesii, both species; Cattleya Bob Betts, a hybrid of C. Bow Bells X C. mossiae, a hybrid and a species; Cattleya Bruno Alberts, two hybrid parents, C. Joan Manda X C. Souvenir de Louis Sander.

The second term is a collective epithet but is printed in Roman type (not italics) and is a fancy name and not a Latinized name. Instead of being called a collective epithet, which confuses it with terminology for natural hybrids, the man-made or artificial hybrids may be designated by the word "grex" which is Latin for flock. Therefore, the collective grex name or grex epithet of a cultivated man-made hybrid includes the genus name and the grex epithet or the name of that flock of seedlings from the same two parents. Easy enough?

The genus may indicate one or more genera in the parentage, not necessarily in the same generation as there are, of course, only two parents per plant. But through the generations there may accumulate as many as four (or more) genera in the ancestry and they all show up in the conglomerate name.

Brassocattleya (Brassavola and Cattleya) is bigeneric (two genera). Add Laelia and it becomes trigeneric, Brassolaeliocattleya. But add Sophronitis and the quadrigeneric name becomes Potinara.

The genus name, however compounded, is followed by the grex name. This may be followed by a cultivar epithet to distinguish an individual (and divisions of this individual) from the rest of the flock.

Anytime any two parents are used, the seedlings receive the same name as the first time it was registered. Every time C. mossiae and C. warscewiczii are mated the seedlings are all Cattleya Enid since Veitch named this cross in 1898.

If you make a cross of any two parents that has not been named and registered, you may name and register it with the International Registration Authority, the Royal Horticultural Society in London.

Examples of hybrids with cultivar names are: Cattleya Barbara Billingsley 'E. J. Small'; Laeliocattleya Bernice Farrell 'Sweetheart'; Brassolaeliocattleya Gladys Lines 'Terri Bates'; Sophrolaeliocattleya Paprika 'Valentine'; and Potinara Gordon Siu 'Potentate.'

The mericlones offered for sale are all vegetative divisions of hybrid plants with cultivar names. Note that in usual conversation the word "variety" is used instead of "cultivar" but it is confusing as only botanically distinct forms of species or natural hybrids are varieties. Variety does not apply to man-made hybrids. Cultivar is a compound word of "cultivated" and "variety" and applies to a variety of a plant under cultivation. However, a jungle collected species which is grown in cultivation and awarded is given a cultivar name.

So the mericlones carry the grex (flock) name and the cultivar epithet to indicate which clone (individual plant) of the original flock has been meristemmed: Blc. Norman's Bay 'Lucile'; Blc. Norman's Bay 'Gothic'; Slc. Falcon 'Alexanderi.'

In addition, orchid names may be followed by initials which indicate awards won by that particular plant. See Chapter III. Examples: Cattleya skinneri alba 'Foster' C.C.M./AOS; Lc. Mem. Maggie Hood 'Boynton' A.M./AOS; Slc. Jewel Box 'Ruby Light' H.C.C./AOS.

Lc. Kathryn Leahey (Lc. Targate x Lc. Bonanza)

Lc. Cecile Simmons (C. Nigrella x Lc. Twinkle Star)

CHAPTER VI

CHROMOSOMES COUNT

Pick up any orchid catalog and along with the descriptions of the plants offered you will see words like "tetraploid," "polyploid," "triploid," or perhaps such symbols as 2n, 4n, and other strange descriptions.

Not Greek at all, these terms and abbreviations have to do with the cell structure of the plants (the science called cytology), and they are important to you because they tell you something about the character or the quality of the plants concerned.

Every plant and animal is made up of cells and within the cells are chromosomes. The chromosomes carry the hereditary units, the genes, which determine the specific characteristics of that individual. In the case of plants the qualities include flower color, size and shape of blooms, rate and type of plant growth, blooming season, and many other factors.

People have chromosomes, too. Every cell in the human body normally carries 46 chromosomes. Twenty-three were contributed by each parent. When there is an abnormal number, the individual is not normal. Mongoloid children have 47 chromosomes. And it is believed that chromosome defects are responsible for some miscarriages and a high percentage of mentally retarded individuals.

The number of chromosomes varies with the species or genus. A normal cow has 60 chromosomes in every cell in its body. A rat has 42; a lily 24; and a fruitfly 8.

The normal number of chromosomes for most Cattleyas is 40. Actually that is the diploid number, and 20 is the haploid number, as each cell has one set of 20 chromosomes from each parent, hence twice 20 is 40. These plants are called diploids, and the abbreviation is 2n. This refers to the number of sets and is called the level of ploidy.

Unlike people, orchids (and other plants) with a greater than normal number of chromosomes are, instead of being afflicted, often finer and more desirable than the diploids.

Orchid plants with twice the normal number are called tetraploids (4n). In Cattleyas this is 80 or 4 times 20. Tetraploids and triploids may have larger and heavier leaves, and while the flowers may not be larger they are always heavier. The superior substance influences form, keeping quality, and other qualities. Knowing that two parents are tetraploids of good quality generally indicates that the seedlings will be of good quality because tetraploids pass their double numbers of chromosomes on to each succeeding generation. Chromosomes retain their characteristics from generation to generation.

If a 2n plant is crossed with a 4n plant seedlings will receive 20 chromosomes from one parent and 40 from the other and the resulting plants are triploids (3n) with 60 or three times the basic number. Triploids generally have fine flowers but are often sterile and difficult to breed. It is sometimes possible to pollinate a triploid with a plant that is very fertile. The famous Hawaiian hybrid, Cattleya Rembrant 'Tenney' was a triploid but nobody knew that back in 1938 when all efforts to breed with it failed until it was crossed with a tetraploid Lc. Pasadena. The progeny, Lc. Rosa Kirsch, were pentaploids (5n). Triploids may be propagated asexually by division or by meristem culture.

There are hexaploids (6n). Polyloids is the general term for plants other than diploids, poly meaning many.

You don't hear much about aneuploids, plants with uneven (41 or 39) chromosome numbers. They are usually the result of mating plants whose chromosome numbers are only partially compatible and generally of diverse genera. If the cross takes, the seedlings are likely to be "off-beat," different from each other and different from the parents. Their chromosome number, flowering and growth habits being unpredictable.

The genes in the chromosomes carry all the characteristics. One that is easy to follow is color.

Genes carry dominant and recessive traits, and the geneticists work these out with formulas according to the laws of chance. Thus they can

Blc. Ranger Six 'A-OK'
(Blc. Nacouchee x
C. Empress Bells)

Blc. Nacouchee 'Margaret' A.M./AOS
(Blc. Headon x C. Estelle)

Blc. Osiris Bay (Blc. Osiris x
Blc. Norman's Bay)

Bc. Heatonensis A.M./RHS
(Brassavola digbyana, a species, x C. Hardyana, a natural
hybrid)

Blc. Miami Sunset 'Mary Estelle'
A.M./AOS.

tell you from a mating of two proven parents which traits will be dominant.

For example, Cattleya dowiana is in the background of many lavender cattleya hybrids because it enriches flower color. The yellow of C. dowiana is recessive, and if crossed with a homozygous purple, the purple is dominant and so all the flowers of the first generation seedlings are purple. A dominant gene and a recessive gene for color from each parent paired off and purple is dominant. (If the purple is heterozygous, there could be yellow in the first generation.)

In the next generation, however, as the pairs segregate with two dominants together and two recessives together, there could be a certain number of yellow flowers.

On the other hand, yellow in laelias is dominant and is being used more and more in breeding with cattleyas to get yellow blooms.

White, which is a lack of color, is recessive, so a white cattleya crossed with a more dominant color results in all colored flowers. And sometimes crossing two albino cattleyas gives purple, as in the case of C. mossiae 'Wageneri' X C. warscewiczii 'Firmin Lambeau.' The resulting C. Enid seedlings are all purple. But semi-albas (white Enids with purple lips) are achieved by using other varieties of the parents.

Color is only one characteristic. Plant size, vigor, floriferousness, season of bloom and other qualities are inherited from dominant and recessive traits. In plants used for breeding for the first time it is difficult to know which traits will be dominant, but in long lines of breeding the characters can be fairly accurately predicted.

I once had a yellow half-Persian cat who mated with a black Tom and always had four kittens: one yellow, one yellow and white, one of three colors, and one solid black. But I later had a black cocker who was one of a litter of three black puppies born of a honey blonde mother.

Mendel's law determines the ratios and behavior of the dominant and recessive genes in individuals.

This is the classic example. If you mate a gray rabbit (indicated AA for dominant gray color) with an albino white rabbit (indicated aa because the white is recessive), the first generation rabbits are all gray with Aa genes. Cross two of these rabbits and you get (on an average) three grays to one white, the genes pairing like this: AA, Aa, Aa, (all three gray), and aa, the white one.

Bc. Mount St. Helens (Bc. Deesse x C. Helen Durfee)

The formulas go on, like 9:3:3:1 for combinations of two independent pairs of characters in the second generation, and so on.

You can't expect to buy 4 orchid seedlings and get three lavenders and one yellow even if the ratio is thus. The percentages hold with flowers, but there are thousands and thousands of seeds in one cattleya pod, and if all were grown to flowering the formulas would work out. But since thousands of seedlings or seeds from any cross are discarded or die along the way, who knows which ones they were?

Counting chromosomes is done with cells from a growing area (generally a root tip) where cells are dividing and the chromosomes can be distinguished. The cells are stained, put under a microscope, and the chromosomes, which look like sticks, dots, or a handful of worms, painstakingly counted. Each one is smaller than 1/1,000 inch, but each chromosome may carry thousands of genes in orderly arrangement. Every time a cell divides the chromosomes divide so each cell in the individual is identical.

This is a fascinating study, and if you wish to pursue it further, you can consult an encyclopedia under headings: Cytology, Heredity, Chromosomes, Genetics or Mendelism.

Sophronitis coccinea, the parent of many reddish hybrids.

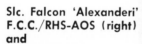

Slc. Falcon 'Alexanderi' F.C.C./RHS-AOS (right) and

Slc. Lindores F.C.C./RHS (below) are both descended from Sophronitis coccinea (syn. S. grandiflora)

▲ **C.** Penang 'Iridescent' **H.C.C./AOS** (**C.** bowringiana, a bifoliate species, x **C.** Nigrella, a unifoliate
hybrid)

◀ Cattleya Hybrida (a natural
hybrid, **C.** guttata x **C.** loddigesii)

C. Lutata (**C.** luteola x **C.** guttata) ▶
a primary hybrid

CHAPTER VII

POTTING

Cattleyas and their relatives that grow in the wild are perching plants. They grow on trees, shrubs or rocks and wrap their roots around their supports. The velamen layer (outside) of the roots has an adhesive quality that sticks like Scotch tape to any surface, and an absorbent ability to take up water and nutrients like a sponge.

Cattleyas grown in cultivation are generally confined to individual pots although some are grown in baskets or on slabs. More about containers later.

When to Repot

Since the sympodial plant grows by moving forward, it will eventually reach the rim of the container. Therefore, the plant must be repotted into another, perhaps larger, container so the roots and rhizomes remain inside the pot.

There are two determining factors as to when repotting becomes necessary. One, when the plant outgrows its pot and the new bulb and new roots will extend over the rim. Two, when the potting material begins to deteriorate and compact so there is not enough air in the container, when the mixture becomes sour or too acid for good growth, does not drain rapidly, or is invaded by snow mold.

Most of the potting mediums in use today will last for two years and so the custom is to choose a container that will support two years' growth, usually two new pseudobulbs.

Vigorous hybrids may need repotting more often. Seedlings in desirable growing conditions may need potting every year. Small plants removed from flasks are planted several to a pot, called a community pot, until they are big enough for individual thumb pots or larger.

Assume you have bought a mature cattleya hybrid in bloom and the flowers have wilted from age. The bulb which flowered rests right at the rim of the pot and when the new eye begins to grow it will climb over the edge of the pot.

In commercial collections repotting is generally done when plants are moved from the flowering house back to their growing positions as this makes for assembly line handling. In small amateur collections, however, it is possible to treat plants individually and time the repotting to the growth of each plant.

We know that growth begins at different periods for different plants and roots appear in the cycle according to their ancestry. Some roots show when the new lead begins, some after it has developed.

Some hybrids, notably those with Brassavola digbyana in their background, make a new lead which grows to full height before showing a new root. Obviously the plant is operating with old roots and to disturb it by repotting during or prior to growth of the new bulb might hinder it because of damage to the old roots.

Other hybrids put out roots from the base of the new lead almost as soon as the eye elongates. If the last bulb is at the pot rim, the new roots will be over the edge. Thus repotting should be done quickly so the new roots go down into the new pot in fresh medium.

I am of the opinion that the best time to repot each plant is at the very moment that new roots appear at the base of the new growth. You must be both quick and careful. New roots are brittle and easily broken. If you repot when they are less than $\frac{1}{4}$ inch long you can repot without damage and they will grow into the new potting mixture. If you let them get a couple inches long, you can hardly repot without breaking them, causing a setback. A plant must have an active and efficient root system to grow.

C. Graniris (C. granu-
losa x C. Iris)

Cattleya forbesii, a species.

Epidendrum Silly (E. ciliare x E. atropurpureum var. roseum)

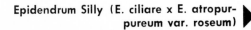

At an orchid show, anything
goes!

Epidendrum stamfordianum has
small yellow flowers dotted with
red

Cattleyopsistonia Leona 'Tommy Vickers' A.Q./AOS (Broughtonia sanguinea x Cattleyopsis ortgiesiana)

Laelia flava 'Gloedeniana'

Epicattleya Vienna Woods
(C. guttata alba x Epidendrum
mariae)

Epidendrum Mem. Young C. Lott
(E. tampense alba x E. mariae)

How to Repot

The first step is the choice of a container. If you expect this plant to grow in the new pot for two years without repotting again, the pot must be big enough to hold two more bulbs ahead of the current new bulb.

Using a pot much larger is not economical because it takes more space and more potting mixture. Further it is subject to overwatering because it does not dry out quickly in the center.

You may not need a larger pot. You might divide the plant into two divisions or cut off the back bulbs for propagation or discard.

Stop here and read from the Propagation chapter the section on Division, then decide about cutting your plant into pieces. Also read in the Problem chapter about sterilizing pots and tools.

Just remember the front lead should have at least three bulbs with leaves to support it.

Put drainage material such as crock (broken bits of clay flower pot), pebbles, screen wire, or a plastic footed disc over the bottom hole to keep it from clogging up.

Remove the plant from the old pot and carefully shake or pull off the old potting mix without damaging the roots.

Then divide the plant, if it needs it. Inspect it all over for pests and diseases. Remove the old sarongs carefully and look for scales beneath them.

Some of the old roots will remain with the back bulbs. Others which look brown and lifeless will come with the front divisions. DO NOT CUT OFF NOR SHORTEN OLD ROOTS.

Recent research at the University of Florida using radioactive phosphorus proved that roots three or four years old absorb and translocate water and nutrients even faster than new roots.

The old method, still used by many growers, is to cut off old roots to within three or four inches below the rhizome. Now we know these roots can function efficiently and they are needed to support the plant, especially while new roots are getting established.

1. Time to repot. New roots are over the side.

2. Push potting material down at rim and work it inward to avoid injuring bulbs.

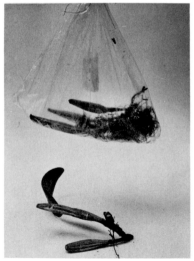

3. Tie up plant with plastic wire so each bulb stands separately.

4. Put rootless back bulbs in a plastic bag with damp moss until they begin to grow.

Rodney Wilcox Jones in one of the greenhouses at Broadview.

Cattleya Margaret Link 'Bernie Wood', semi-alba or white-colored-lip.

Cattleya Mary Ann Barnett 'Luxembourg Waltz' A.M./AOS a fine white in the Bow Bells group.

Take the front division you are ready to repot. Hold the back end of it against the rim of the pot and make sure enough space remains forward of the newest bulb for two more bulbs. If it is growing in two directions, check out both. Hold it so the rhizome is about half an inch below the rim.

Work your potting material down around the roots under the rhizome and into the pot. If you use a potting stick or tool, push at the rim of the pot and not against the bulbs or you might break the good eyes. When the mixture is firm the plant should be secure. Fasten a stake to the rim and tie the bulbs in place, wrapping the wire or string individually around the neck of each bulb in turn. Plastic wire from discarded telephone cables is excellent orchid wire. Position the bulbs upright as individuals so each one gets as much light as possible. Don't tie them in a bunch like celery. If you leave two long wire ends at the first bulb you will be able to tie up the new bulb when it grows tall enough.

If the plant is inclined to rear up above the potting mixture, use a pot clip which hooks over the rim and holds the rhizome firm on the top of the potting medium. Do not bury the rhizome in an effort to make the plant secure. It should creep along on top of the medium.

The potting mixture should be damp when it is used, and newly potted plants should be set in a humid, rather shady place for a few days if possible.

The Potting Mediums

Cattleyas are epiphytes which need a potting medium with characteristics similar to the natural conditions under which they grow.

Durability: the mixture should hold up for about two years.

Drainage and aeration: roots need air and water, but water should run off and not stand in soggy compost. Oxygen must be present in the potting mixture or roots will die.

Nutrient availability: the character of the potting material must be such that roots can absorb nutrients from it. Some mixtures contain -nutrients, you have to add fertilizer to others.

But there is a chemical characteristic that has to do with what the roots can absorb. The term pH defines the acid or alkaline character of the potting mix. Cattleyas seem to adjust to a wide pH range, but a figure near 6 seems to be preferable. This is slightly acid, as pH 7 is neutral on a scale of 0 to 14. The pH of the mixture changes according to the character of the water, and in most situations after a year the pH of the mixture might be down to pH 5, which is perfectly acceptable.

If all the plants in a collection are suffering from poor growth, an analysis of the water or potting mix might indicate an extreme pH range.

The medium should retain nutrients for a reasonable time yet let them be washed out so the accumulation of salts does not become dangerous.

Ease of handling: since potting is a tedious chore, any material that is easy to work with is desirable. Time and labor (yours or hired) are factors to consider.

Reasonable cost and availability: orchids are grown all over the world and growers try to find materials that are inexpensive and available without shipping large quantities of bulky material for great distances.

OSMUNDA — The roots of the cinnamon fern and the royal fern (Osmunda cinnamomea and Osmunda regalis), handsome ferns with six foot fronds, provided the favorite orchid potting material for many years. The wiry black roots or soft brown roots of these ferns are dug with difficulty, cut into chunks, and washed free of mud. The ferns grow in wet ground in North and South America, the West Indies and Eastern Asia.

The advances of civilization have made osmunda more and more scarce and inaccessible and the cost of labor to dig it is becoming prohibitive.

But osmunda is a very satisfactory potting material for orchids. Plants will grow in it without additional fertilizer, as it contains small amounts of nitrogen, phosphorus, potassium and minor elements. It holds up a year or two, and has both air spaces and water retentive qualities. The pH is around 5.0.

In Europe sedge peat and sphagnum moss are sometimes combined with osmunda to reduce the cost per volume at a ratio of 2 parts osmunda to one part sphagnum and coarse peat. Some European growers pot with the roots of the polypodium fern (Polypodium vulgare) or polypodium and sphagnum moss.

FIR BARK — In use for about 10 years, practically all the orchid growers on the West Coast of the U.S. pot in bark or bark mixtures.

Kiln dried Douglas fir (Pseudotsuga taxifolia) or white fir (Abies concolor), along with other species, are the choices. The bark is left over when logs are debarked, and it is chopped and screened to remove small particles and sawdust.

Bark comes in various sizes chosen according to the size of the plant and the pot.

The pH range is about 4.0 to 6.0 depending on the type wood.

Some growers use a 7 to 3 mixture of medium grade bark and redwood chips and claim it is easier to water, makes fertilizer more available and reduces snails and fungus.

Bark should be moistened before using as it is difficult to get wet if entirely dry. See instructions for fertilizer in Chapter II.

TREE FERN — The fibers of various tree ferns from Hawaii, Mexico and the West Indies are excellent potting material for orchids. The Hawaiians began using tree fern in volume during World War II when it was impossible to import clay pots and osmunda from the mainland. They call it hapuu.

Tree fern is kiln dried and screened and is available in grades of fine, medium, coarse and little chunks. It comes in slabs, round and square totems, baskets, balls, and monkeys.

Tree fern drains well, holds nutrients, and does not disintegrate quickly. In tropical climates where orchids are grown outdoors and rainfall is heavy, pack the fibers vertically so drainage is quick. The pH is about 4.6.

Tree fern is very easy to pot with and can be worked into place with the thumbs or with a potting stick. Some growers mix tree fern with other materials. Some work a bit of decomposed manure in with it.

Plants in tree fern welcome regular applications of balanced fertilizer, and watering when the fern begins to dry out.

ASSORTED MIXES — There are numerous mixes, varying in ingredients.

One of these is a mixture developed by George Off and called the Off mix. The formula is 57% fir bark, 32% coarse peat moss, 5% redwood fiber (Palco Wool), 6% coarse perlite. To each 10 cubic feet of this mix add 4 lbs. bone meal, ½ lb. superphosphate, ¼ lb. ureaform nitrogen ·(Uramite), and 1½ lbs. greensand (Glauconite, not sand at all).

The New Jersey mix is a modification of the Off mix developed by Rutgers University and several New Jersey orchid nurseries. It works out to a 7-1-1-1 or a 6-2-1-1 formula depending on the coarseness of the peat moss. The large number is fir bark ($\frac{1}{4}''$ to $\frac{3}{4}''$) and succeeding numbers peat moss, redwood bark and coarse perlite.

Separate the redwood fiber through a shredder or coarse screen. To each cubic foot of peat moss add 1 lb. pulverized limestone. Then mix peat moss, fir bark, redwood, and perlite. To each 10 cu. feet of this mix add another $\frac{2}{3}$ lb. pulverized limestone; 3 lbs. bone meal or 1 lb. 20% superphosphate; $\frac{1}{2}$ lb. processed tankage; $\frac{1}{2}$ lb. 5-10-5 fertilizer.

Fertilize every second watering with 2 rounded teaspoons of 30-10-10 in 5 gallons of water, first watering the pots with clear water.

Lc. Portia Dane (C. Portia x Lc. Peter Dane).

Both of these mixtures are trouble to put together but you can buy them already mixed. The New Jersey mix drains faster and has more air spaces than the Off mix.

FIRED CLAY — In warm wet climates where plants are grown under lath and must dry out quickly, fired clay materials sold as Solite are proving useful. These do not build up fertilizer salts, nor encourage mold or fungus.

Because of the rapid drainage between the marble sized chunks (this is not untreated clay soil), plants may be overpotted if there is room on the bench for large pots. Fertilizer is suggested at 20-20-20 every week if the temperature is warm.

OTHER MATERIALS — Pumice, coconut fiber, redwood fiber, cork slabs, and other materials that are available easily are used in many areas for potting orchids. There are always new materials being tried, and some growers have success with sheet moss and fern moss in dry areas, with plastic pellets, large particles of vermiculite, and other things. There are frequent articles in the A.O.S. Bulletin on potting materials, and several are discussed in the issue of November 1965.

Containers

CLAY POTS — The most used containers are clay pots in sizes from $1\frac{1}{2}$ inches to 12 inches, the measure being the distance from rim to rim across the top at the widest part (the diameter of the circle).

Some pots are shallow (called bulb pans), some have vertical slots in their sides, which increases drainage. All must have adequate drainage holes, and some growers knock larger holes in the bottoms. It is impossible to knock slits into the sides. Pots must be baked that way.

Ceramic pots are rarely acceptable for planting as they lack drainage, but can be used for temporary pot covers.

PLASTIC POTS — These are very popular with some growers and the square ones fill a bench without wasted space. Close staging cuts down evaporation and watering frequency, but the schedule must be regulated to prevent overwatering.

Since plastic pots are not porous, as are clay pots, and no air can reach the roots through the sides, the potting mixture must be sufficiently porous for air to penetrate from the top.

If you have some plants in clay and some in plastic, group them on your bench and water according to the dryness of the medium, which will vary with type and size of pot.

BASKETS — Wooden baskets are generally used for vandas and orchids of other types but can be used for large cattleya types if you have space for them. One Florida orchidist has an enormous plant of Cattleya skinneri alba in a 40-inch wooden basket which received a Certificate of Cultural Merit from the American Orchid Society (91 points) when it had 49 spikes and 314 flowers. The basket is very shallow, about six inches deep, and as the plant gets bigger the sides of the basket are removed and extended. Large plants are apt to remain wet in the center of large containers unless they drain rapidly.

SLABS — Slabs or logs of tree fern or driftwood are useful where orchids can hang up and can be very decorative. The plants don't need repotting until the material disintegrates or they smother it. A round ball of tree fern the size of a basketball (or even a baseball) covered with plants of Brassavola nodosa is a delight when blooming in an open space. Hairpins are used to secure plants to fern until the roots anchor them. Slabs need frequent water and high humidity as water runs off rapidly.

MISCELLANEOUS CONTAINERS — All sorts of containers can be used. Handsome bonsai pots (if they have drainage holes), half coconuts, wire baskets, and other things are possible if you manage the water and air at the roots. Fancy containers are lost on crowded benches and take extra space, but if you have display space and can keep the plants happy with individual attention, they add interest.

POT COVERS — There are many materials and designs for covering clay pots while plants are on display in the house. And an orchid in bloom is a wonderful flower arrangement right on the plant. Check gift shops at home and when you travel for raffia, metal, ceramic and other covers. Set pot and all inside the cover, but remove plant and pot from the cover to water and drain it in the kitchen sink as needed during its indoor stay.

CHAPTER VIII

PROPAGATION

Propagation means multiplication. Two for one, by division. Perhaps thousands from one (selfed) or two (crossed) parents. Or thousands from one by meristem propagation.

Division of Mature Plants

When you are repotting, decide if the plant is to be left in one piece or if it can be made into two or three plants. This will be determined by the number of bulbs, the amount of space you have, and the value of the plant. If the flowers are of so-so quality, one plant is enough. Discard surplus bulbs.

If, however, the flowers are of excellent quality, and the plant has six full-grown bulbs and is making one or two new leads, you may wish to divide it into two plants of three bulbs each. If you have space on the bench or windowsill for two plants. One large plant takes up less room, and one large plant with two or three leads in bloom is more spectacular than two small plants each with one stem of flowers.

On the other hand, once you get past six or eight-inch pot size, it takes time to dry out the compost in the center and it is too easy to overwater.

When you get the plant out of the pot, shake off or gently pull off the old potting mixture and check over the plant. Remove all the old brown sarongs carefully so as not to damage the eyes beneath.

Then count the bulbs, allowing at least three mature bulbs to support each new lead. If the plant is making leads in more than one direction, see if you can allow at least three bulbs behind each one. It may not divide in this manner yet. Then count the remaining bulbs for possible back bulb propagations.

Any set of bulbs must have at least one good green eye in order to grow. Check the sketch on page 11 for the location of the eyes. If the eyes are all brown and shriveled, probably damaged by scale, there is no point in expecting new bulbs to grow from them.

Cut through the rhizome at the points you have selected. Pull the pieces apart gently, so roots will untangle and go along. Pot up the divisions that have active leads. If the back bulb piece has roots for anchorage, pot it up. If there are no roots, put it in a plastic bag with a handful of damp osmunda, sphagnum, Spanish or peat moss. Tie the top tightly, attach a name tag, and hang the bag in a warm shady place like at the side of the greenhouse bench. When the back bulb shows eye or root growth, pot it up.

These divisions will all result in exact duplications of the original plant. If it carried a varietal name or an award, the divisions carry it, too. Back bulbs may not bloom for two or three years.

Orchids From Seeds

Growing orchids from seeds is a tricky business because the seeds are tiny and have no cotyledons like the two halves of a bean that are reservoirs of food.

Orchid seeds must be sterilized and planted in entirely sterile conditions and grown in bottles containing nutrient solution to nourish them. In time, the tiny seedlings are transferred to community pots, then to individual pots, and in four to seven years should begin to bloom.

There are thousands, maybe millions, of seeds in each orchid pod, all as fine as dust. There are variations in the flowers that result. See Chapters on Heredity, Hybridization and Chromosomes for explanations.

A batch of hybrid seedlings can be quite varied. Nobody can predict which of the seedlings will have the best flowers. Some may combine the worst qualities of both parents. And nobody can grow all the seedlings from one pod to blooming size. There are too many.

If you have two orchids you want to cross, consider first if you have the space and patience to grow a number of seedlings to maturity. Do you have space for a quantity of 5-inch pots of all the same kind, and time to repot and care for them as they are growing to that size?

If you have limited space but want to try seedlings, buy some flasks or community pots of several different crosses and grow them to flowering.

Before you make a cross consider if the parents are of good quality and if the combination would be worthwhile if the seedlings inherited the best traits from both sides. Check the hybrid list to see if this cross has been made and named, and inquire if it turned out well or was disappointing. Of course, you can remake any cross, but not name it if it has been registered.

There are thousands of orchid hybrids in the world already. If you want to try your hand at hybridizing, put your time and effort into a combination of traits that has promise.

TO POLLINATE THE FLOWER: Nature's ways of transferring pollen from one flower to another are beyond belief in their ingenuity. Check book list for a splendid book on orchid pollination, and reread pertinent paragraphs in Chapter III.

Bees may pollinate your flowers for you, but since you do not know the identity of the pollen parent, you can't register chance seedlings of orchids as you can chance seedlings of camellias. And bees don't tell. Cattleyas are pollinated by bees. Ants, butterflies, humming birds, flies and moths pollinate other flowers in the group.

Self-pollination indicates the pollen from one flower is put onto its own stigma, or the pollen from another bloom on the same plant is used.

Cross pollination is the use of two parents, which may or may not be of the same genera.

To carry a seed pod a plant must be in robust health and kept growing. Remember that it must have enough reserve growth to support the pod above that it needs for maintenance and normal growth. No need to

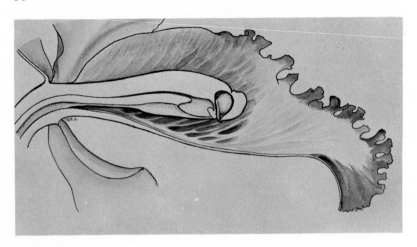

put pollen onto the flower of a sickly plant or a seedling blooming for the first time.

Recheck Chapter III for a description of the column which contains the reproductive parts. And locate on the sketch above these three parts of the column. The pollen grains, like pinheads, behind the anther cap at the front on the underside. Next, a partition called the rostellum which prevents self-pollination. Behind that a cavity called the stigma which receives the pollen.

To pollinate a cattleya flower, take a toothpick or wooden matchstick and insert it beneath the pollen grains and pry them loose. Hold a piece of paper beneath, as you may drop them. If the anther cap comes loose, discard it. (See sketches.)

Then insert one of these grains into the stigma cavity and push gently until it sticks by itself. You will do this all with one flower on one plant if you are self-pollinating, or transfer the pollen to a second flower to make a hybrid. Label pollinated flowers at once.

THE POD: In a few days, if the pollination took, the petals and sepals will collapse and the ovary will begin to swell. The ovary is that portion of the flower stem immediately behind the bloom and as it develops the flower, which has served its purpose, withers and dries up.

If you wait for the pod to mature and split, you may lose some of the seeds. The better way is called green pod or embryo culture, by which the pod is harvested before it ripens and splits but at some speci-

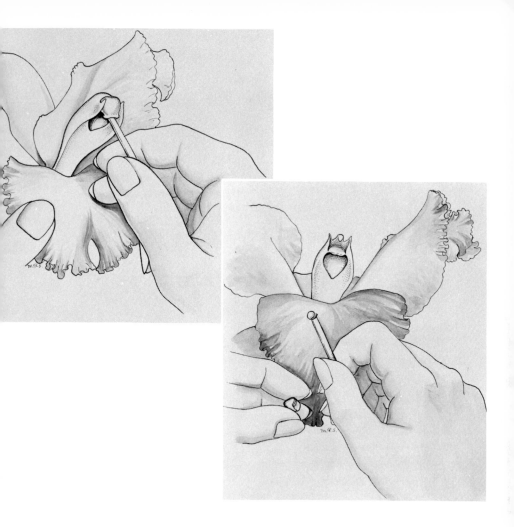

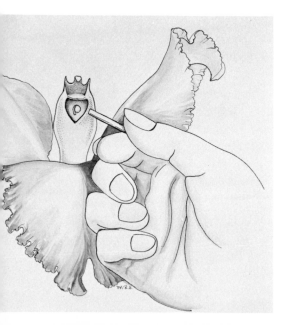

To pollinate a cattleya-type flower:

1. Remove anther cap with match or toothpick.
2. Attach pollen to match for transfer.
3. Insert pollen in stigmatic cavity of same flower or another flower.

Seed pods form where stem (pedicel) was. Withered flowers hang onto ends of pods.

fied time when the seeds will germinate. A larger percentage of seedlings generally results from this technique. The timing varies with genera and species. The time for harvesting cattleya pods is about 180 days after pollination, but is less for some species. It is about 100 days for most of the epidendrums, except E. conopseum which is ready in 60 days and E. atropurpureum which requires 150-160 days.

SOWING THE SEED: You can buy a complete flasking kit from some orchid supply houses, or you can buy the culture medium and get bottles and stoppers locally. Of course you could mix your own medium, but this is a tedious chore for a small operation and requires precise measurements in small quantities, so you are better off to buy the formula and mix with distilled water and heat it exactly as prescribed by the manufacturer.

You can buy flasks for this purpose, or use flat-sided glass quart milk bottles or 4-oz. square-sided glass baby bottles.

The following procedure is the method used by Gordon Vickers of Jacksonville, Florida, who does his flasking on the kitchen table using a plastic dry-cleaner's bag as his "flasking case."

Rinse out new bottles with hot water. Boil used bottles 30 minutes. Rinse bottles with a Clorox solution (1 part Clorox to 10 parts water) and rinse this out with distilled water or boiled rain water. Invert bottles on paper towels to drain. (Clorox is a bleach that is 5.25% sodium hypochlorite.)

Make stoppers of absorbent cotton, rolling cotton to fit bottle necks tightly with part of the wad protruding above the top.

Prepare the agar according to directions. Have tools ready and steri-

Gordon Vickers uses a plastic bag for a sterile flasking case and works with one hand inside and one hand outside.

lized. Spoon agar from cooking pan into a 2-cup pitcher. Into each bottle pour enough agar to cover bottom one-half inch deep. Wipe off any agar that spilled on the inside of the bottle neck. Insert stopper.

Put bottles into a pressure cooker and cook at 15 pounds pressure for 10 minutes. Let the steam out gradually or the stoppers will blow. Take out bottles and put in position until agar jells. This means upright baby bottles or flasks remain upright, milk bottles lay on their sides.

An alternative method is to sterilize bottles in a turkey roaster. Put them on a rack in the roaster, put water under the rack enough to just touch the bottles. Do not stopper bottles or they might break. Cover the roaster with its own lid or with aluminum foil and bake 35 minutes at 350. Let cool until bottles can be handled. Insert caps and put in position to jell.

Have ready a clear plastic bag, a large rubber band, a clean cotton rag, a stainless steel knife with a dull point, a stainless steel iced tea spoon, a stainless steel stiff wire with the ends bent into loops and a plastic bottle with a top for misting containing Clorox and water at 1 part Clorox to 10 parts water.

Put some of the Clorox solution into the cup. Put the rag and the tools into the solution.

Cut off the blossom end of the seed pod (the withered flower still hangs on.) Scrub the outside of the pod with soap and water, then wring out the rag and wipe the outside of the pod. Put the pod inside the plastic bag.

Wipe tools with rag and put inside the bag. Spray the outside of the bottles lightly all over with the Clorox solution in the mist bottle and spray the cotton caps lightly especially at the rim.

Squeeze out the rag and wipe off the bottles and put them into the plastic bag. Spray inside the bag until it is damp all over. Spray your hand and arm and put it inside the bag up to the elbow. Having first put the rubber band over your arm above the elbow, pull it down and fasten the bag securely around your arm, gathered so there is no opening.

Using one hand outside and one inside, work with the bottles and tools to plant the seed. The atmosphere inside the bag is sterile, along with everything in it.

Take out stoppers and wipe bottle necks with the rag. Split pod in half with the knife and put down half of it. Use knife to slowly scrape a small amount of seed into the bottles. If you use upright baby bottles or flasks, scrape right into the neck of each bottle. If you use milk bottles that lie flat, scrape seeds into the spoon, insert it into the bottle and use the wire to help distribute seeds over the agar.

Put down the knife and the pod when all bottles are filled and cap the bottles. Remove from bag and label at once. Cover cotton stoppers with rounds of freezer paper tied with string around the bottle necks. Put them in a warm place where there is light but not direct sun. Mr. Vickers puts his bottles on the kitchen windowsill where the temperature is 72 degrees. He pastes white paper across the glass behind the bottles to cut down the light. About 200 foot candles is desirable light at first. It may be increased to 300 or 400 foot candles and then more as the plants grow.

If you flask a ripe seed pod that has split open it is necessary to sterilize the seed. Dissolve five Chlorazene tablets in 4 oz. distilled water.

Put some in a test tube with the seed, cover with a rubber stopper and leave for 15 minutes, shaking frequently. Use the wire to dip into the tube and transfer seeds to the bottles, spreading seeds over the medium.

In place of a plastic bag you can work with your hands inside your oven preheated to 200 degrees. Do one bottle at a time, removing cap and inserting seeds and recapping.

Orchid nurseries use cases with glass tops, fluorescent lights, filtered vents, and holes for hands to go into attached gloves. Seeds must be sown in sterile conditions or mold will grow and all will be lost. Mold might appear in spite of all precautions.

If you want to make a cross but not go to the trouble of sowing the seeds, there are nurseries with flasking service.

REFLASKING: When the protocorms begin to show distinguishable leaves and roots, it is well to transfer them to bottles with a different solution, which you can buy for this stage.

Take all the precautions as before except that you will need additional bottles if many seed germinated so you can put fewer in each bottle.

When you have all the sterile materials, including old and new bottles, inside the bag, take stoppers out but don't mix them. Use the spoon to lift out seedlings and the wire loop to separate the clumps and drop them a few at a time into the new bottle. Use the wire to spread them around. Try not to crowd them. They need room to grow.

SEEDLINGS: When seedlings are of sufficient size they are poured out of the bottles, the agar washed off, and the little plants washed in Anti-Damp. Then they are planted in community pots or flats of some fine potting medium. Keep them warm, moist and shaded.

Fine tree fern is one choice for the potting medium. Another is 10 parts seedling bark to 1 part peat moss. There are variations, but the mix should be able to stay moist without being soggy.

Small seedlings can be kept growing as rapidly as possible without the rest periods required by some mature plants to initiate or develop flowers. Acceleration of seedlings is possible by growing them under artificial lights to lengthen the day to 17 hours, but there is not that much rush unless you are a commercial grower.

Pot them ahead to pots of suitable size as they grow. Allow a pot big enough to support one year's growth at each repotting.

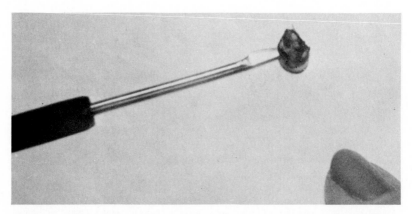

Meristem tissue taken from interior of new lead. This piece will be peeled down to smaller size before being propagated. Thousands of plants can be grown from this tiny bit of plant tissue.

Meristem Culture

Meristem culture is a type of propagation which burst into the news in recent years. Meristem propagations look like seedlings while they are growing up, but whereas seedlings are variable, meristem plantlets are all identical with each other and with the mother plant.

Meristems propagations (called mericlones) are asexual or vegetative divisions and so no element of chance is involved.

The apical meristem of any plant is the growing point. In a chrysanthemum it is the growth bud at the top of the stem. In an orchid it is a tiny piece of tissue deep inside a growing lead. The cells in the meristem have not yet differentiated into those that will become roots, leaves or flowers, but are capable of developing into any of the plant parts.

The tiny bit of meristem tissue for propagation is secured by cutting through layer after layer of tissue to reach this microscopic point. A piece of tissue about 1/25th inch in diameter is removed (excised) under sterile conditions and put into a flask on agar like seeds are planted. The flask is agitated.

You would not think such a tiny piece of a plant could grow into another plant, but actually it can be made into thousands or millions of plants.

As alike as peas in a pod are these three mericlones blooming for the first time. These are plants of Laeliocattleya Culminant 'La Tuilerie.' For close up of flower see page 2.

The tissue develops into a pinhead size ball of green cells called a protocorm. The cells in the protocorm are not yet differentiated into leaves and roots, and before they do, the protocorm is cut into pieces and each piece then becomes another protocorm. The protocorms are cut again and again and the process can go on indefinitely. But when the cutting ceases and the protocorms are allowed to grow, they put out roots and leaves and grow into individual plants.

The culture is as for seedlings, from flasks or bottles into community pots or flats, and on into individual pots.

The flowers of mericlones are exact replicas of those of the mother plant. If the mother plant had a varietal name or an award, the mericlones have them, too, because they are divisions just as back bulbs are divisions.

The meristem process was applied to orchids at first for the purpose of producing some of the fine plants in virus-free form by Georges M. Morel, a French plant physiologist. Under expert hands and with the utmost care, the tissue can be excised from the mother without becoming contaminated with virus even though the mother plant is known to ᐧbe diseased.

Unfortunately, however, not all mericlones that are grown to maturity are virus-free. Tests have shown one-third of a batch to be contaminated. The virus can be transmitted in the original propagation, in subsequent potting, by insect infestation or careless handling. A mericlone is not immune to virus, but may have started out free of it.

The French nursery of Vacherot and Lecoufle recognized the possibilities for mass production of fine plants by the meristem method and announced in 1964 that they had thousands of mericlones growing in small individual pots and were prepared to meristem plants for anybody. Many plants from all parts of the world have been sent to them to be meristemmed, and many nurseries are doing their own.

As a result, many fine and famous orchids are available to amateur growers at reasonable prices. Whereas divisions of the originals were not only scarce but expensive, now everybody can have divisions through mericlones.

The effect on amateurs is an upgrading of collections, replacing poor quality flowers with fine ones. But mericlones do not replace seedlings, which can be had for newer crosses, and the fun of seeing the first blooms. There are always new trends represented in new crosses, whereas some of the famous orchids that are being meristemmed were first flowered many years ago. Slc. Falcon was registered in 1917 and Slc. Anzac in 1921, but they are still hard to beat and everybody wants them, and can have them now, thanks to meristem propagation.

The effect of mericlones on commercial growers is that cut flowers of desirable color and season can be grown in great and uniform quantities, just like identical roses are grown in quantity.

Do not try to make meristem propagations yourself unless you have the microscopes and tools and are expert at taking care of plants from protocorm stage upward. Only a very fine plant should be meristemmed, and you have to cut off a new lead to get the tissue in the meristem, which may set back the growth of the plant. If you have something that good, it is better to get some nursery to make the propagations for you.

Any mericlone must be grown well for it to produce flowers of its full potential. A mericlone blooming for the first time or a poorly grown plant will not have flowers of equal quality to one that is mature and well grown.

CHAPTER IX

PROBLEMS

Problems of orchids are of three types: insects, diseases, and physiological disturbances.

Before you treat a problem you must identify it.

The insects are the easiest to identify because most of them are visible or their damage gives clues. Insects are persistent and constant vigilance is needed to keep ahead of them.

The illustrations of the pests and their damage look like orchid growers' nightmares, but do not be alarmed. You will never have all of these problems at once, and many of them you will never have. Use the drawings for identification.

Insect controls are given in chart form on page 126. You do not need a different insecticide for each insect, as you will find many of the chemicals listed for several pests and one spraying (repeated as directed) should eliminate the pests that are present.

Regular spraying, probably monthly, with a three-way product containing insecticide-fungicide-miticide should keep the usual problems under control. Orchid nurseries and garden stores sell products formulated for orchids. Most of the three-way mixtures recommended for roses are suitable for orchids.

Special treatment may be needed for unusual problems.

Some of the systemic insecticides, such as dimethoate (Cygon) and Meta-Systox R, are very effective because they are absorbed by plant tissues and remain effective in all parts of the plants for longer periods than contact insecticides on the surface.

All insecticides should be used with caution as many of them are toxic to people, some more than others. Read the label directions entirely and follow them explicitly. If the container directions indicate use of smaller quantities than the chart in this book, by all means use less as the formulation of that brand may be stronger.

Dithio smokes are very dangerous and should be used with great care.

The diseases, particularly the virus diseases, are the most serious because no cure is known yet. The best thing to do is to get the virus identified by a laboratory (probably your state university can do this), and then try not to spread it to healthy plants. Do not panic every time a plant has a leaf spot or a streaked flower as it does not necessarily indicate virus. However, if a plant is positively identified as having virus, destroy it if it is not a very valuable specimen or a stud plant. Many of the fine studs have virus.

Problems of environment such as air pollution, climate, and other factors may be beyond your control. Cultural difficulties suggest that you need to develop a better understanding of your plants and their requirements.

Prevention of Problems

As with problems of any type, avoiding them is easier than curing them. So it is with orchid pests and diseases.

One point is sanitation. Debris encourages pests and diseases. A clean greenhouse or growing area is important. Keep the greenhouse clean all the time, and when warm weather permits move the plants outdoors, a group at a time, and scrub down the glass inside and out with Clorox and detergent, scrub the benches, and clean out beneath the benches.

Remove old foliage as it dies and old flowers as they fade and dead plants as they give up. Old flowers give off ethylene gas which can cause sepal wilt in other flowers. Store your potting materials elsewhere than in the greenhouse in a dry, clean place.

Sterilize your cutting tools between work on each plant because virus is easily transferred by cutting a healthy rhizome with a knife that had cut a diseased plant. The easiest is to wipe them with a solution of 2% formaldehyde and 2% sodium hydroxite (which is 3⅓ teaspoons 40% Formalen and ⅔ ounce sodium hydroxide to one quart of water). The way to do this is to put a small amount of this mixture in a little plastic squeeze bottle with a sponge on top like you use for licking stamps and envelopes. Just pass your knife over the sponge, both sides of the blade, and do the same for any other tools like clippers or whatever. Other methods are to dip tools in boiling water for 20 minutes between plants, or flame them over a propane torch.

Small knives for cutting flowers are available for a few cents each. They are razor blades in plastic handles. One knife is used for cutting each flower stem, then put into a separate container and another one used for the next flower stem. The accumulation of used knives is easily sterilized in the oven.

Sterilize your pots, crocks and stakes before using again. Dip them in Clorox (one part to 10 parts water). Rinse them thoroughly in clear water. If you fail to rinse well, the bleach may injure the roots. Some hobbyists scrub their pots by hand with a brush and soapy water, soak them in Clorox, and then soap and rinse them in the kitchen dishwasher. Beware of putting dirty pots in the dishwater.

Nature will sterilize your pots for you if you set them out in the open sun for a couple of weeks. If old roots stick to the insides, scrape these off first. A better method is to scrub the pots in Clorox, rinse well, and then set them in the sun.

FRIENDS: You have many friends at work for you if your plants are in a greenhouse or outdoors. Spiders, lizards, toads, frogs, lady beetles, praying mantis and many other critters work for you day and night.

Isolate new plants until you inspect them thoroughly. Never accept a sickly plant because it is a bargain or a gift. It might introduce some problem that would attack some better plants in your collection.

Weak plants that are poorly grown are more subject to ills than healthy vigorous plants. Lack of light, poor air circulation, too much or not enough water and fertilizer, low temperatures, all these things make for weak growth and invite problems.

Problems of the Green Parts
Pseudobulbs and Leaves

The Insects

Keep a close watch on your plants. If you have a small collection you can pick up and examine each plant from time to time. Take good notice of the ones on the back row, and the ones that hang up. You may be inclined to overlook them.

Check particularly the underside of the leaf, as many pests congregate there. Check the crevice where the leaf, sheath and bulb join, and behind old sheaths at this point. Also around the growing eye which has a notch behind it even before it begins to swell.

Pest controls are given in a chart on page 126.

SCALES may be hard scales with round hard bodies like brown or white pinheads, or soft scales that look like white powder. They appear in large numbers and multiply fast in the warmth of heated greenhouses or tropical climates. Constant vigilance is required, but scales can be controlled with today's chemicals. Neglect is responsible for serious infestations in orchid collections.

The white scales collect under strings that tie up plants, but I have not noticed them beneath plastic telephone wires since I have been using these for plant ties. Scales collect beneath the sarongs that cover the pseudobulbs, either while these covering leaves are still green and the bulbs still growing, or after bulbs are mature and the sarongs turn brown. Scales collect around the ankles of pseudobulbs, especially under the eyes. Scales can destroy an eye so new growth is impossible and thus kill the plant.

A favorite method for amateurs is to mix up an insecticide such as malathion and rub off visible scale with a toothbrush. The danger in this method is in breaking the skin of the plant by rubbing too hard with a stiff brush, or even breaking off the growth eye by trying to dig out scale behind it. A systemic is faster and more efficient. I find a good way to combat scales is to keep a plastic bottle with a push-button top that makes mist filled with insecticide and handy on the greenhouse bench ready for instant spraying. Then at first sight of scale, it is eliminated and not left to multiply until a more convenient time when a whole batch of spray is mixed.

Armored scales have hard shields over their bodies. Soft scales look like white powder or flour. The common orchid scale, Boisduval scale, looks soft because the males appear in cottony masses but the females are round, flat armored pinheads.

All scales are sucking insects which pierce the plants with their needle-like mouthparts and suck out the juices.

Scales on the underside of a leaf may not be noticed until the upper surface begins to turn yellow in the areas above them. Scale damage never regains its green color and the infested areas may turn black even after the scales are eliminated. A fringed scale from the Caribbean makes pits in the plant surfaces.

Since not all insecticides are effective against the adults and the crawlers, too, or cannot penetrate the shields to reach the eggs or crawlers beneath the female scales, repeated applications at specified times may be needed to eliminate the next generation.

MEALYBUGS are really soft scales which when mature are oval with white powdery coverings over their bodies. As crawlers they are light yellow, smooth insects. Some adults have long tails. Each adult female lays 300 to 600 eggs, so to keep from being overrun with mealybugs, get rid of them as fast as they appear.

Mealybugs are sucking insects which inhabit the axils of leaves and crevices. They produce copious amounts of honeydew which attracts ants and forms a medium for growth of sooty mold fungus.

If you see only a few mealybugs, dip a match wrapped in cotton into alcohol (nail polish remover is good) and touch the pest with it. For larger infestations, control as for scales.

If you grow soft-leafed foliage plants in your greenhouse with your orchids, check them for mealybugs which inhabit things like coleus, crotons, ferns, fuchsias, gardenias, poinsettias and strelitzias. Plants outdoors near the greenhouse may be hosts to mealybugs, among them chrysanthemums, geraniums, English ivy, pineapples, bananas and tomatoes.

APHIDS or plant lice come in many colors—black, green, pink, yellow, red, brown and what have you. They may be winged or wingless.

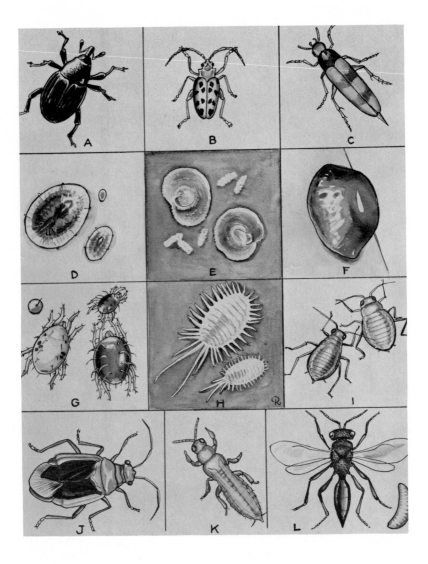

Green Part Pests and Their Damage

A. Weevil
B. Beetle
C. Leaf Miner
D. Brown scale
E. Boisduval scale
F. Hemispherical scale
G. Mites (Red spiders)

H. Mealybugs
I. Aphids
J. Orchid plant bug
K. Thrips
L. Cattleya wasp (fly)
M. Grasshopper
N. Caterpillar

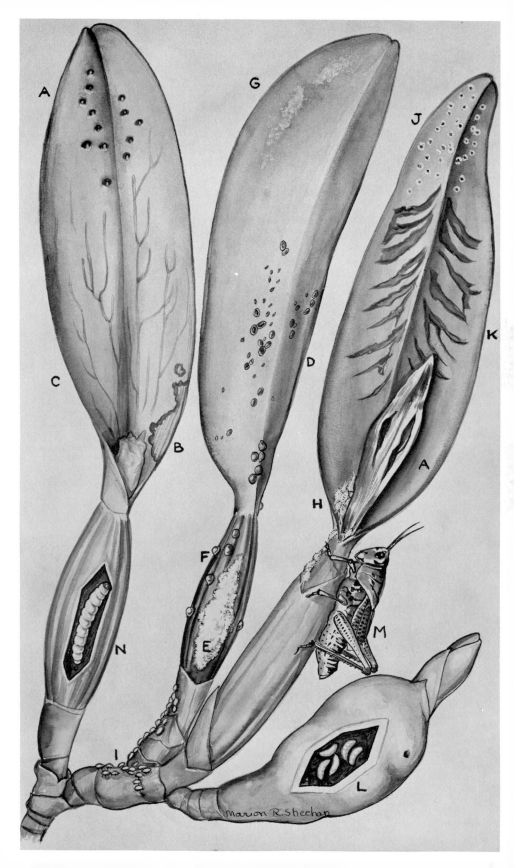

In warm climates living young may be produced continuously without an overwintering stage. There are a great many types of aphids on a great many plants including orchids.

They have piercing mouthparts and they suck out plant juices and cause stunting, deformation and curling of leaves and flowers. They secrete honeydew which encourages sooty mold fungus, and they transmit diseases from one plant to another.

Typical aphids have soft, pear-shaped bodies, six legs, antennae, and segmented bodies and beaks with four needle-like stylets. They vary in size but mostly are visible though very small, about 1/50 of an inch.

Aphids are called greenflies or black flies in some places.

MITES, red spiders, or spider mites are serious pests in hot, dry situations. They are tiny relatives of chiggers, spiders, scorpions and ticks which look like dots of pepper, generally red.

In severe infestations, fine webs may be seen spun across the undersides of leaves, especially when webs glisten with water. Not all spider mites spin webs.

Mites are of various colors and with many types and names: two-spotted mites, false spider mites, etc. They are all sucking insects that cause leaves to look silvery and pitted where they have drained out the juices. There may be a new generation in 10, 20 or 30 days, or every five days, if the temperature is above 75°F. Each female lays 100 to 200 eggs.

Mites increase rapidly in dry hot situations—outdoors, indoors, or in a greenhouse. Frequent inspection is needed to find them before all the color is drained from a leaf.

Mites are not insects but animals, therefore not all insecticides are effective against them. Miticides may be needed for control. Mites have increased enormously since DDT was developed as DDT kills off their natural predators and seems to make plant tissue more susceptible to mite damage. If you use DDT in the garden or greenhouse, you must use a miticide, too. Repeated applications of miticides in 7 to 10 days are necessary to control the next generation.

GRASSHOPPERS of all sizes chew on orchids. The big lubbers we have in Florida gnaw at the cattleya leaves or the sides of the pseudobulbs. The damage shows jagged threadlike edges like torn cloth.

CATTLEYA WASPS, called CATTLEYA FLIES have been all but eliminated by the use of DDT, but crop up now and again. The female inserts her eggs into new pseudobulb growth. Upon hatching, the larvae remain inside the plant and feed there.

This causes the infested bulb or lead to swell up to abnormal size and to be unusually pointed at the end like a bamboo shoot, and to stop growing. The larvae change into black wingless flies $\frac{1}{8}$ inch long and emerge from tiny holes or cause the bulb to burst open. The life cycle is 50 to 60 days.

You are not likely to see the flies, but if a lead is growing with obvious abnormality, cut it open to see if there are tiny worms inside. If so, cut off the infested bulb and burn it. If you throw it on your trash pile, the larvae will mature into flies anyhow and lay eggs in other plants.

WASPS other than Cattleya wasps of various small species called chalcid wasps are pests of orchids. Some attack the green parts, others the roots, depending on the species.

BEETLES are problems in some areas. In Thailand one called the cucumber beetle attacks orchids, but it is not a striped beetle like the one we call cucumber beetle in the Deep South U.S.

WEEVILS are destructive. They feed on flowers and leaves, and the larvae feed inside roots, pseudobulbs or leaves, having been inserted through punctures. These $\frac{1}{8}$ inch shiny black beetles can be identified because their heads are prolonged into beaks or snouts. The cattleya weevil has white markings on his back, but a solid black one called the orchid or dendrobium weevil also feeds on cattleyas.

ORCHID PLANT BUGS are true bugs, about $\frac{1}{8}$ inch long with orange to black bodies and steel-blue and black wings. They have piercing and sucking mouthparts and suck juices out. This causes yellow raised circular areas to develop, or irregular white stippled spots to appear on undersides of leaves.

Young bugs resemble adults without wings. The Brazilians call them "little red orchid roaches."

THRIPS have rasping, sucking mouthparts, are more often a problem on flowers than on foliage.

LEAF MINERS tunnel between the leaf surfaces and so are hard to reach with insecticides. They are rare on orchids, more common on azaleas and other shrubs. Systemic insecticides might control them.

CATERPILLARS may attack foliage on the surface. A South American pest lives inside the pseudobulb. A systemic insecticide might be effective.

The Diseases of the Green Parts

VIRUS is a great problem in orchids just as it is in people. And in both instances, unidentified maladies are called "virus" whether or not.

The sanitation suggestions at the beginning of this chapter offer some protection against infiltration and spread of virus in your collection. Some identification that the problem is a disease and not a pest is necessary for treatment.

CYMBIDIUM MOSAIC VIRUS is a serious problem of cattleyas, epidendrums, laelias and bigeneric hybrids as well as cymbidiums and phalaenopsis. The symptoms vary but generally include dark red or brownish purple spots that are sunken and make the leaf rough. The spots may begin along the veins and unite to form long streaks. As they run together a whole leaf becomes dark. There may be brown or purplish-black ringspots on the undersides of the leaves or on both upper and lower surfaces. On reedstem epidendrums the ringspots may be round or oval, brown or black, located on undersides of leaves.

Older leaves on cattleya hybrids may drop prematurely, giving the plant only one or two front leaves to carry on the photosynthetic process.

TOBACCO MOSAIC VIRUS "O" STRAIN is not too harmful. There may not be visible evidence of this virus, or there may be light yellow patches on the leaves. Often plants have tobacco mosiac virus and cymbidium mosaic virus both.

These virus diseases are usually transmitted through cutting flowers or dividing plants using a knife on a healthy plant that was used on a diseased plant. Viruses are not transmitted by wind or water but by a wound or opening on a plant touched with the juice from an infected plant. Aphids and roaches can transmit viruses from plant to plant.

The best diagnosis of these virus diseases is made by a virologist in a laboratory. The juice from a suspect plant is rubbed onto a sensitive host plant (certain cassias, gomphrenas, or daturas) and if the reaction is positive the host will become spotted in a certain number of days.

Virus is not known to be transmitted through seeds, so seedling plants are free until infested by external sources. Likewise, meristem plantlets are assumed to be virus free if the meristem has been carefully excised from the parent, but these plantlets may become infected as they grow by careless handling. Just because a plant began life as a meristem (mericlone) does not guarantee it to be free of virus all its life, and a number of them are infected.

The estimate is that about five percent of the mature orchid plants in cultivation are carrying a virus. Virus is found in wild plants, too.

If you buy plants that are without visible symptoms and you make every effort to avoid spreading disease, your collection should be reasonably healthy but probably never 100% virus-free.

FUNGUS diseases attack cattleyas and allied orchids. Fungi are plants themselves, originating from spores that are carried on wind or water. The spores settle on some host plant, germinate like seeds, and extend their roots (called mycelium) into the host plant. You have to cut off the infected area to eradicate the fungus.

BLACK ROT AND HEART ROT are encouraged by cool temperature and high humidity. Community pots are susceptible to this in the form of damping-off and a whole pot may be destroyed in a week. The fungus is spread by splashing water. Try to water early in the day so foliage is dry at night.

Plants that have moving air and are not crowded together are less subject to attack.

Symptoms on the leaf are purplish brown or black areas outlined with yellow which spread over the entire leaf. If the pseudobulb is infected first, it turns purplish-black and the leaf falls off, perhaps without withering. The rhizome may be the source of infection if cut with an unsterile knife.

PYTHIUM BLACK ROT is most prevalent in warm weather or warm climates where temperatures are over 70 degrees F. Probably all the intergeneric cattleyas are susceptible. This disease starts at the rhizome and works upward.

The first signs are small water-soaked spots on the leaves which turn dark purplish-black, with the same yellowish advancing margin of the above disease.

If the atmosphere is humid and warm, infected areas are soft but if the air is dry the discolored sections may be dry and brittle. The spread is so rapid that progress is visible daily. It is most often spread through the rhizome by cutting with an infected knife. The bulb may rot at the base and topple over.

Control of black rots: Use Tersan 75 as a spray on neighboring plants to keep it from spreading. Dip infected plants, pot and all, in a 1:2000 solution (¾ teaspoons to 1 gal. water) of Natriphene for one hour, repeat in three to seven days if needed. In severe cases remove plant from pot, cut off infected areas and dip what is left. Treat with Ferbam, Zineb or Captan by spraying undersides of leaves where stomates are (leaf openings) that permit spores to enter.

ANTHRACNOSE FUNGUS may attack leaves, pseudobulbs or flowers. The organisms enter injured spots such as sunburned leaves and spread from there. Plants injured by sun, cold, chemicals, too much fertilizer or otherwise in poor health and without good roots may be attacked.

Sunken brown discoloration first appears, having a definite line of demarkation from healthy tissue. Spores show up later like pinpoints. Sunken spots may be light green or yellowish.

Cut off and burn infected areas and spray cut edges with Ferbam, Captan or Zineb.

Check your conditions for excess sun coming directly on the injured plant if this is the cause, or check out your fertilizer mixtures as too much nitrogen can cause damage allowing for entry of the disease. If a plant is generally unhealthy and not producing roots and sturdy new growth, examine it for weakness by pests, soggy potting medium, or otherwise poor culture.

RUST FUNGUS is prevalent in some countries, and some countries and some states in the U.S. have regulations prohibiting entry of plants infected with rust.

One rust fungus has been reported on plants of Cattleya dowiana, and C. dowiana var. aurea, and two laelias. Two or three other rusts are prevalent on some epidendrums.

Generally the rusts show up as orangy patches on the undersides of the leaves, circular in pattern, small at first then becoming larger rapidly until the entire lower leaf surface is covered. The infected leaves appear chlorotic and yellowish in the same patterns on the upper surfaces over the spots.

No cure is known, and the fungus grows inside the leaf as well as outside. Inspection of the lower leaf surfaces of any plants which appears to discolor on the top surface is advised. Cut off and burn the infected leaf or destroy the entire plant if rust is definitely diagnosed. Spraying neighboring plants with Fermate may help to prevent spread of the disease. Keep an eye on newly imported orchids of cattleyas, laelias and epidendrums, although you may be sure the quarantine people culled any that showed rust symptoms.

LEAFSPOT may appear on Cattleya-type orchids on young seedlings of community pot and slightly larger size. The disease may appear on larger seedlings but is not so severe and generally does not cover nor kill the entire leaf.

The small seedlings may appear to be infected with spider mites because tiny dark spots appear on the undersides of the leaves with corresponding yellowish spots on the upper surfaces. Close examination will show the pinprick spots of the fungus are raised, while the mites cause sunken spots. However, leafspot on larger seedlings appears as irregular yellow spots which become black and sunken with age.

Control of this leafspot (Cercospora odontoglossi) is not yet determined as it is a fairly recent problem. Captan, Ferbam, and Zineb are effective.

SOOTY MOLD FUNGUS is familiar to growers in the areas where gardenias, citrus, mangoes and avocadoes grow. This fungus grows in the honeydew secreted by white flies and aphids. It appears as black film on the leaves. Control the insects and wipe off the fungus.

Sooty blotch and flyspeck are also surface problems, one a film and one tiny specks, which thrive on plants grown shady and cool. Provide more light and warmth, and wipe off the discoloration.

BACTERIAL DISEASES include brown spot and soft rot.

BROWN SPOT (Pseudomonas cattleyae) is rather common on cattleyas but not too destructive but is a serious problem of Phalaenopsis seedlings. It occurs in wet overcast weather.

Older leaves develop sunken black spots which rarely spread to other leaves even on the same plant. Treat by spraying with Tersan 75 or dipping plants in a 1:2000 solution of Natriphene for 60 minutes.

SOFT ROT spreads rapidly and smells bad.

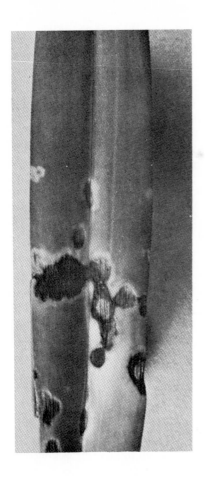

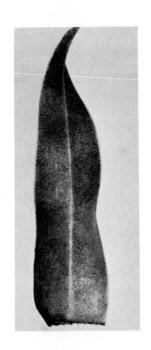

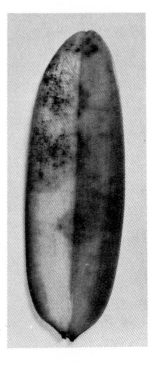

Above left: Bacterial brown spot (Pseudomonas cattleyae) on cattleya leaf.

Above right: Leafspot (Cercospora odontoglossi) on underside of cattleya seedling leaf, community pot size.

Lower right: Same leafspot on underside of a nearly mature cattleya hybrid leaf.

Cut off and destroy infected leaves immediately. Disinfect the bench with formaldehyde or Clorox. If you throw away the plant, throw away the pot and stake, too. Treat cut surfaces with a Tersan paste.

Miscellaneous Problems of the Green Parts

When leaves fall off, it may be normal procedure. After their life span, old leaves from back bulbs drop from the plant as new bulbs and leaves grow. This quite often happens in the fall of the year as days are getting shorter and growth is slowing down. It is no cause for alarm if only the back leaves fall. Wait for them to drop. Breaking them off is likely to tear the tissue of the pseudobulb.

Also a product of aging is shriveling of older pseudobulbs. We know from experiments that their roots remain active and useful even as new roots grow on the front but there comes a time when old roots decline in vigor and the bulbs become wrinkled longitudinally and the leaves fall off. If bulbs near the front begin to show wrinkles, then check the condition of the root system. If roots are in soggy compost, injured by disease or too much fertilizer, or smothered by mycelium fungus or snow

Brassavola perrinii

mold, then they may not be functioning sufficiently to provide moisture and nutrients to the green parts. Repotting may solve the problem.

Problems of the Flowers

The Insects

Some of these pests have been described under problems of the green parts.

APHIDS congregate on buds and flowers and you can spot them as tiny bumps generally near the tips of the buds after buds emerge from the sheath. Aphids cause flowers to be crippled, of uneven color, or to fail to open. They can carry virus diseases.

THRIPS are tiny slender insects usually less than 1/25th inch long and no wider than a small sewing needle. They are prevalent outdoors in warm weather and come into the greenhouse as fast as you can eliminate them.

Thrips are barely visible except that where there's one there are many. They have wings, too small to see, and piercing mouthparts which scar the flowers. Occasionally thrips are found on new foliage. Thrips-infested blooms and leaves are irregular in surface and color, sometimes curling or otherwise deformed.

Control of thrips on garden plants, such as roses, and removal of grassy weeds near the greenhouse, helps keep down the infestation. Some are carried by wind and arrive from nowhere. They are too small to be screened out.

SNAILS AND SLUGS are very partial to orchid flowers and appear in the dark of night to feed upon the flowers and buds. Slugs can be identified by their slimy trails. These creatures are seldom seen, but if damage from one is evident, take drastic control measures for there are probably many others lurking around.

Everybody recognizes a snail, which may be the size of a pinhead or as big as an edible tree snail. A slug is a snail without a shell.

Snail or slug damage generally results in grooves cut in wavy patterns into the flower or bud surfaces. Some of the bait preparations are effective, but the creatures have been known to build up an immunity. Better control may be achieved with a drench if the pests hide in the pots.

If ground cover plants are grown under the benches, you must control snails and slugs that enjoy the cool, damp conditions down there.

ANTS rarely do actual damage to orchid flowers except for pollinating some of the very small blooms. Tiny sugar ants may be seen at the back of the flower where it joins the stem eating the drops of honey.

Ants keep company with aphids, mealybugs and scales and sometimes move these pests from one plant to another, spreading the problems and possibly diseases as well.

CATTLEYA WASPS, (CATTLEYA FLIES) are seldom encountered, may lay eggs inside flower buds as well as pseudobulbs, and the larvae will be observed when the bud tries to open or falls from the plant. Destroy it by burning and inspect other plants closely.

COCKROACHES like to live in warm greenhouses, come in from outdoors in warm climates. They chew on flowers at night, eating away great hunks from the edges. They hide by day in the orchid pots or warm, dry and dark corners, under debris, and in basket plants.

A bottle cap is a splendid container for dry roach poison placed on or next to each flowering plant. Control can never be relaxed because more roaches always come from somewhere. If you encourage chameleons or other lizards to live among your orchids, the roaches will be fewer.

CRICKETS, also night feeders, are fond of flowers and said to be partial to white ones.

BEES AND WASPS do no physical damage to flowers except to pollinate them or disturb the pollen which causes the flower to fold up prematurely.

RODENTS: FIELD MICE AND CITY MICE (AND RATS) get into the greenhouse and eat flowers or pollen. Quite often they break a flower bud off its stem by their weight when attempting to reach the pollen or eat the honey where the bud joins the stem. SQUIRRELS may break off buds and eat them.

Screens and closed greenhouses deter these pests, but in warm climates where houses are open or plants grown in slat houses or outdoors, small containers of poison will deter the rats and mice. Squirrels will eat sunflower seeds in preference to orchids if you supply same.

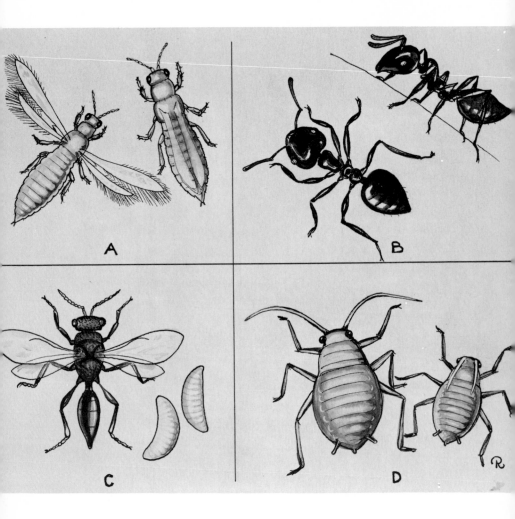

Flower Pests and Their Damage

A. Thrips
B. Ants
C. Cattleya wasp (fly)
D. Aphids
E. Snail
F. Slug

G. Cockroach
H. Cricket
I. Bee
J. Wasp
K. Mouse
L. Squirrel

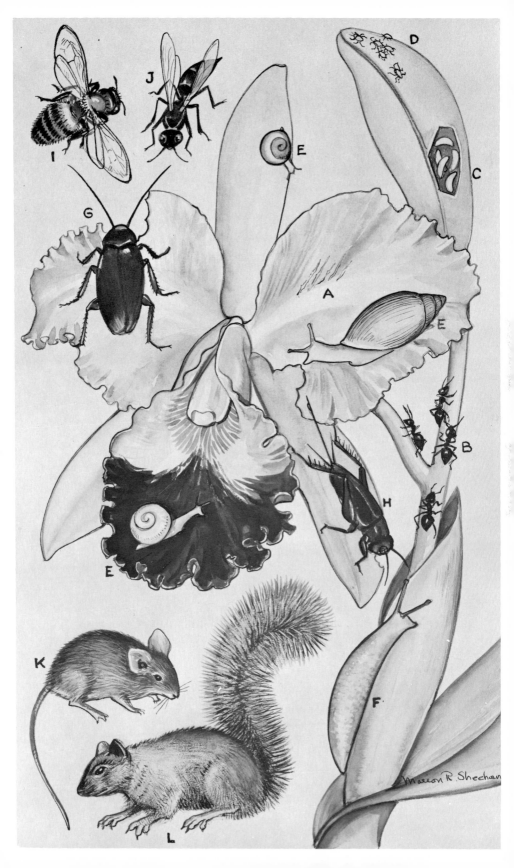

The Diseases of the Flowers

VIRUS in flowers show up in the color pattern. Two diseases are known in cattleyas and their hybrids.

CATTLEYA COLOR-BREAK in mild form shows distorted color patterns, more pronounced on the first bud to open, and repeated with each flowering. Marks on the sepals or petals may be darker or lighter than the basic flower color, but flowers are not distorted in shape or thickness.

A severe cattleya color-break virus disease shows patches of color in the flower parts, darker or lighter than normal and flowers may be distorted or crippled. Lighter and darker mottling may show up on leaves, which may be deformed in shape. There may be raised dark green areas in longitudinal ridges.

Flowers with color-break are of no value. If in doubt about it being a virus, or if only one flower is deformed or discolored, let the plant flower again. If it shows up the second time, throw it out.

Color-break can be transmitted from plant to plant by insects or tools. It often accompanies cymbidium mosaic virus.

BOTRYTIS disease, which is common on cattleyas and phalaenopsis during cold, damp weather, is petal blight. It causes small round spots on the flowers, usually as tiny as pinpricks at first becoming larger like freckles and more numerous rapidly. This common fungus disease can ruin a crop of flowers in no time. Cut off and destroy all infected blooms immediately before it spreads to other blooms in the house. If you keep the air circulating even on a cold night by cracking a ventilator at the far end of the greenhouse from the heater, the moving air will keep the moisture in the air from settling on the flowers and help to prevent this kind of spotting. A new material named Tutane gives promise.

BLACK ROT fungus may attack flower buds. See Green Parts.

ANTHRACNOSE may cause tiny brown spots to appear on old flowers, which enlarge, run together and destroy the whole flower. To keep flowers from spotting, spray for a few seconds with Natriphene 1:2000 plus a drop or two of mild liquid detergent. This will not cure spotting, but help to prevent it on flowers when the disease is present in the green parts. This treatment may be used to help prevent Botrytis.

Of course, flowers on plants that are unhealthy due to insects, diseases or poor culture are not going to be up to their full potential, and the basic problem should be solved in order to produce better flowers.

Left: Botrytis cinera, petal blight.
Right: Color break virus

Miscellaneous Problems of the Flowers

Environmental problems may be hard to cope with.

AIR POLLUTION of cities causes buds or newly opened flowers to shrivel and fall off, and is a serious problem at certain times of the year where air pollution is heavy. Greenhouses near expressways may suffer in flower production because of the fumes of the vehicles.

SEPAL WILT may occur, characterized by dryness beginning at the tips and spreading as brown, tissue-papery areas inward on the sepals.

A minor sort of aid can be supplied by keeping the humidity as low as possible during periods of high air pollution. The oxidizing pollutants in the air dissolve faster in a moist atmosphere, so unless the air is naturally heavy with moisture (quite often it is), don't water or spray until the wind changes and the pollution is lessened.

Another possible item is to avoid fertilizing plants in bud or flower with a high nitrogen fertilizer during periods of high air pollution, as it has been reported from the New York Botanical Garden that nitrogen apparently absorbs and translocates the pollutants into the plants.

FLOWER WILT, BUD DROP OR SEPAL WILT may be caused by rapid changes of temperature from hot to cold, overheating, cold drafts, or other such conditions.

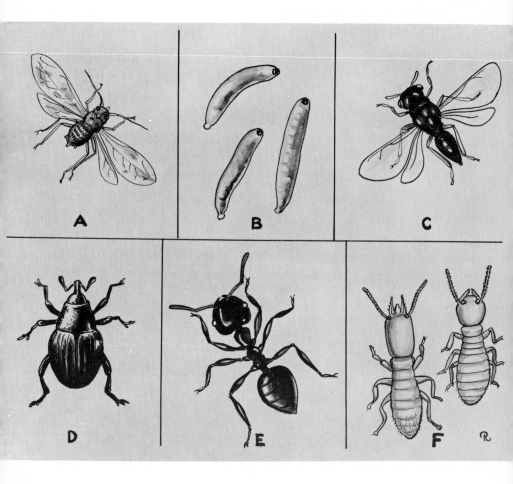

Root Pests and Their Damage

A. Woodlice or slaters
B. Fungus gnats
C. Root flies
D. Orchid weevil
E. Ants
F. Termites

G. Snail
H. Slug
I. Caterpillar
J. Cockroach
K. Cricket
L. Millipede

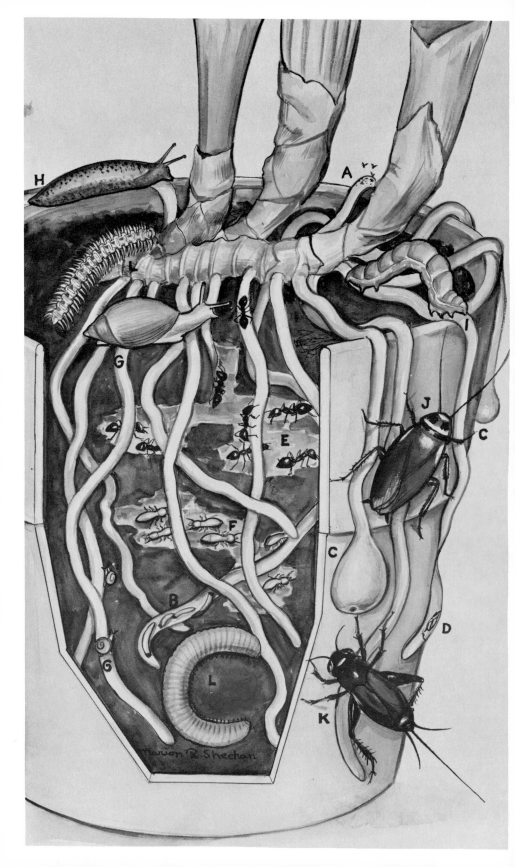

Marion R. Sheehan

Problems of the Roots

The Insects

ANTS AND TERMITES often nest in orchid pots, coconut shells or baskets. You may not know they are there until you douse a plant with water and some come to the surface or you find a telltale pile of sawdust beneath the pot. These may be little ants or big ones to $\frac{1}{2}$ inch like the carpenter ant we have in the eastern United States.

Termites have straight bodies and ants have nipped-in waists. Termites don't like light and make tunnels to travel through. Ants or termites may be controlled by dusting the surface or drenching the potting medium.

Orchids must have an affinity for ants and termites as people who collect plants from the wilds are always finding ants nesting in or around the orchid plants.

SNAILS AND SLUGS, previously described hide in the pots and do damage to roots or emerge and chew the green parts and blossoms. Tiny bush snails (pinhead size with brown shells) are extremely destructive to roots, especially seedlings grown in bark. Mixing redwood fiber with bark repels them to some extent. When repotting, roots should be examined for snails, and dipped in a solution of some systemic such as Zectran.

ROOT WASPS attack roots like Cattleya wasps attack pseudobulbs. They are quite rare and can be spotted as they cause swelling of roots on top of the compost or outside the pots. Swelling occurs next to the root tips. The best control is to cut off the infested roots and burn them.

WOODLICE OR SLATERS are nocturnal winged insects, minute in size, that feed upon the tips of new roots. They breed in litter and rubbish, so if your greenhouse or growing area is kept clear of trash you probably will not be troubled. Roach or ant baits are effective, or you can make traps by hollowing out the insides of apples or potatoes and putting them near infested plants.

CATERPILLARS may be a problem in tropical countries. One called the semi-looper is an Asian problem that chews new root tips and new shoots.

COCKROACHES AND HOUSE CRICKETS, already mentioned, may eat roots at night.

ORCHID WEEVILS, already described, may deposit larvae in new roots.

MILLIPEDES, called thousand-legged worms, are grey, brown or pinkish brown round worms with many segments and generally less than 400 legs, not 1,000. They feed on decaying organic matter, may live in pots and eat orchid roots. If you see them, they will be coiled up like springs.

FUNGUS GNATS are not gnats but flies, about the size of mosquitoes. The maggots feed on decaying and damp organic matter. Some are harmless but other species may feed on orchid roots.

The Diseases of the Roots

FUNGUS DISEASES previously described may attack green parts or some of them attack the roots or rhizomes.

PHYTOPHTHORA, BLACK ROT of leaf and heart rot, may also attack at potting level causing footrot. Generally infection enters when a rhizome is cut with an infected knife during repotting.

PYTHIUM BLACK ROT begins in the green parts but advances into the roots and kills the plant. The infection may enter the rhizome on a cutting knife.

RHIZOCTONIA (Pellicularia) is a destructive root rot which attacks plants from community pot to old plants. It is usually present as a brown mycelium in the potting medium especially if it has gotten old and soggy and drainage is poor. Even recently repotted plants may have it if drainage is inadequate.

The roots may be lost before any above ground symptoms are noticed, when pseudobulbs and leaves become shriveled yellow and twisted. Sometimes the rot will progress into the rhizomes and partly up the pseudobulbs.

Remove a suspect plant from its pot and shake off the potting material. If the plant has live roots, treat with Fermate. If it has no live roots, dip

Fusarium wilt infects orchid roots and causes green parts to turn yellow and pseudobulbs to become shriveled and twisted.

it for 5 minutes in Terrachlor 1 tb. per gallon of water. Repot with extra drainage in fresh material.

FUSARIUM WILT is a root disease of cattleyas, allied hybrids and bulbous epidendrums.

It is characterized by plants which slowly decline anywhere from three weeks to a year after repotting when the fungus infected the plant through the cut rhizome or roots. Thin, yellowish leaves and twisted pseudobulbs are aboveground symptoms that all is not well with the roots. A purplish circle in the rhizome is a symptom which may extend an inch or more up the base of the pseudobulb. There is as yet no chemical for control. If the plant is valuable, cut forward of all the purple discoloration and repot in fresh material. Sterilize osmunda, which can carry Fusarium spores, with a 4% formalin drench.

SNOW MOLD is a fungus which attacks not the plants but the potting material. It is a saphrophyte which grows in the potting material and shows up as white powdery growth on top of the pot or at the cracks in the sides, which means it is all through the pot.

It harms the orchids by covering the roots, rhizome and even the pseudobulbs at the base depriving roots of air and moisture and causing them to suffocate.

Dry the plant out before dipping it in Shield 10% mixed at the rate of 1 ounce to 4 gallons of water. Remove plant from pot and remove by hand as much of the fungus and potting material as possible. Then dip, repeat in two weeks.

Chameleons and toads are your friends. They eat more bugs than you will ever see. Try to keep them happy and many of your pest problems will vanish.

Note: DDT and some of the other chemicals have become unavailable since first publication of this chart. Read labels on available chemicals to find specific controls for these problems.

PEST	INSECTICIDE AND FORMULATION	DOSAGE TO 1 GAL. WATER	100 GAL. WATER	REPEAT
ANTS	Chlordane 40% WP	2½ tb.	2½ lb.	
	Chlordane 42-46%	2 tsp.	2 pt.	
	Apply Chlordane to benches, ground under benches, interior walls. Don't get on plants.			
	Diazinon 25% EC	2 tsp.	2 pt.	
APHIDS	Dimethoate (Cygon 2E) 23.4% EC	2 tsp.	2 pt.	4 weeks
	Lindane 20% EC	1 tsp.	1 pt.	
	Lindane 25% WP	1 tb.	1 lb.	
	Malathion 25% WP	4 tb.	4 lb.	
	Malathion 50-57% EC	2 tsp.	2 pt.	
	Meta-Systox-R 25.4% EC	1 tsp.	1 pt.	4 weeks
	Diazinon 50% WP	1 tb.	1 lb.	
	Dibrom vapor (1 oz. per 10,000 cu. ft.)			
	Dithio smokes			
BEETLES	DDT 50% WP	2 tb.	2 lb.	
	Lindane 25% WP	1½ tb.	1½ lb.	
	Diazinon 25% EC	2 tsp.	2 pt.	
CATERPILLARS	As for Beetles			
CATTLEYA WASPS (CATTLEYA FLIES)	Diazinon 25% EC	2 tsp.	2 pt.	8 times at 2 week intervals
	Dimethoate (Cygon 2E) 23.4%	2 tsp.	2 pt.	
	DDT	2 tb.	2 lb.	4-6 weeks

Pest	Treatment	Amount	Frequency
COCKROACHES	See Roaches		
CRICKETS	As for Grasshoppers		
FLIES, BLACK	See Aphids		
FLIES, CATTLEYA	See Cattleya Wasps		
FLIES, GREEN	See Aphids		
GNATS, FUNGUS	Diazinon	1 tsp.	2 lb.
	Lindane 25% WP	2½ tsp.	1 lb.
	DDT 50% WP	2 tb.	2 lb.
	Malathion 25% WP	5 tsp.	2½ lb.
GRASSHOPPERS	Catch them if you can		
LEAF MINERS	As for Thrips		
MEALYBUGS	As for Soft Scales. Or touch with cotton swap dipped in alcohol.		
MILLIPEDES	Diazinon 50% WP	1 tsp.	2 lb.	10-14 days
MITES	Chlorobenzilate 25% WP	1 tb.	1 lb.	7-10 days
	Aramite 15% WP	1½ tb.	1½ lb.	30 days
	Dimite	1 tsp.	1 pt.	
	Ethion 23-25% EC	2 tsp.	2 pt.	
	Ditho Smokes			4 applications—3-4 days apart
	Kelthane EC 18½%	2 tsp.	2 pt.	7-10 days
	Kelthane 18½% WP	2 tb.	2 lb.	
	Meta-Systox-R 25.4% EC	2 tsp.	2 pt.	as above
	also as drench			

Pest	Insecticide and Formulation	Dosage to 1 Gal. Water	100 Gal. Water	Repeat
MITES (Cont.)	Pentac 50% WP	1 tsp.	½ lb.	two applications, 10 days apart
ORCHID PLANT BUGS	DDT 50% WP	2 tb.	2 lb.	
	Malathion 25% WP	4 tb.	4 lb.	
PILLBUGS	Diazinon 25% WP	2 tsp.	2 pt.	
ROACHES	Chlordane 40% WP	2½ tb.	2½ lb.	
(COCKROACHES)	Chlordane 42-46%	2 tsp.	2 pt.	
	(Spray benches, greenhouse walls. Don't get on plants)			
	Diazinon 25% EC	2 tsp.	2 pt.	
	Household roach baits set out on bottle caps on benches as needed			
ROACHES, LITTLE RED	Orchid plant bugs			
RODENTS	Stomach poison locally available			
SCALES				
Armored, Soft and Mealybugs	Dimethoate (Cygon 2E) 23.4% EC (or as drench 8 oz. to 50 gals. water)	2 tsp.	2 pt.	3-4 weeks
	Ethion 23-25% EC plus oil emulsion 97% (do not use on community pots)	2 tsp. 3 tb.	2 pt. 3 qt.	
	Malathion 25% WP	6 tb.	6 lb.	
	Malathion 50-57% EC	1 tb.	3 pt.	
	Meta-Systox-R 25.4% EC	2 tsp.	2 pt.	

Pest	Treatment		
SCALES (Cont.)	Diazinon 25% EC	2 tsp.	2 pt.
	Dithio Smokes		
SLATERS	See Woodlice		
SLUGS } SNAILS	Metaldehyde 15%		
	(dust around pots and benches)		
	Metaldehyde WP or baits		
	(follow label directions)		
SOWBUGS	As for Millipedes		
SPRINGTAILS	As for Thrips		
TERMITES	As for Ants		
THRIPS	DDT 50%	2 tbs,	2 lb.
	Dimethoate (Cygon 2E) 23.4% EC	2 tsp.	2 pt.
	Lindane 25% WP	1½ tb.	1½ lb.
	Malathion 25% WP	4 tb.	4 lb.
	Malathion 50-57% EC	2 tsp.	2 pt.
	Diazinon	1 tsp.	2 lb.
WASPS	See Cattleya Wasps		
WASPS, ROOT	Cut off swollen tips and burn		
WEEVILS	As for Beetles		
WOODLICE	DDT (drench)		

{ 4 applications
3-4 days apart
Repeat 1 month

Hanging Orchids

A heart of clipped palmetto frames two orchids and crystal teardrops which are anchored in space with invisible nylon thread. Hang this from a light fixture over a festive buffet table.

A Christmas decoration of orchids, ornaments, crystal leaves and velvet ribbon. Hang it over a holiday doorway. Both designs by Winni Price.

CHAPTER X

FUN WITH ORCHIDS

Orchids are for fun, and you can have fun with them by sharing them, wearing them, and using them.

One flower in an inexpensive bud vase will give great pleasure to a sick person, especially in a hospital room crowded with big arrangements of flowers because the little orchid can sit on the bedside table. It can convey your congratulations to somebody with a birthday or anniversary, your sympathy in bereavement, or your compliments on a festive occasion.

Nero Wolfe isn't the only man with orchids on his desk. Any executive would welcome one in a vase from you.

There are thousand of people of your acquaintance who have never had an orchid, and your gifts need not be limited to corsages for the ladies. Orchids in vases are welcome by men on any occasion.

Orchids to Wear

Boutonnieres for men are becoming more popular, and there's nothing better than an orchid. Nowdays when all of us feel lost in the crowd, and feel like we are not people but numbers (zip codes, social security numbers, area code numbers, and on and on), a boutonniere establishes individuality.

A waistline corsage of rainbow-colored reed-stem epidendrums. Design by Glad Reusch.

A graceful curved corsage of cluster-type cattleyas backed with net, pearls and a small satin bow.

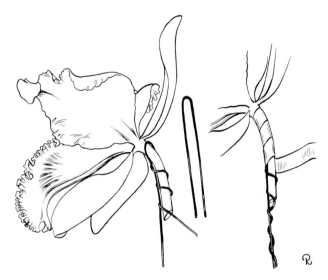

How to wire a cattleya for a corsage. Make a hairpin of corsage wire. Place over stem and wrap one end around the stem and the other end. Cover wire and stem with floral tape which sticks to itself if stretched lightly as it is wound around the stem.

Rodney Wilcox Jones, to whom this book is dedicated, wears an orchid every day. And even in the rush hour mob of Grand Central Station, he stands out from the crowd. Other commuters know his name, and strangers stop to admire his flower. The boutonniere helps to establish him as man of distinction.

There are many small orchids in the Cattleya group that serve well, notably some of the epidendrums and laelias, and with only a few floriferous plants you can have boutonnieres for almost every day in the year.

Try giving them away, too, to the president of a luncheon club, the chairman of the board, or to the boss.

Corsages need not be made of big purple cattleyas with lots of ribbon. For many occasions, the smaller flowers in smaller designs are more appropriate and for many costumes they are more harmonious. You don't have to wait for a holiday to wear or give a corsage. Think of your hostess at a church meeting, somebody in a retirement home on a birthday, or the mayor's secretary when you want an appointment with His Honor.

Wiring a flower stem for a corsage is very easy. (See sketch.) Take a piece of corsage wire of about 24-gauge for large flowers, finer wire for smaller flowers. Form it into a hairpin. Place the curve over the stem back of the flower. Let one side of the hairpin remain straight beside the stem, wrap the other end around and around both stem and wire.

Using a piece of corsage tape, begin at the top and wrap around the stem and wire, stretching it lightly as you go so it sticks to itself.

Finish with a bow of ribbon if you wish. The trick in tying a bow that is fluffy and not flat is to pinch the ribbon each time a loop comes to the center and then to use a separate piece of ribbon to tie around the center of the loops. Twist the piece you will tie with twice through the middle, then knot it over the collection of loops and pull ends tightly. Use these ends then to tie around the flower stem. Don't try to make the bow on the flower. Make it separately, secure the loops in place, then tie the bow around the stem.

For small flowers in the group that have delicate stems, cover stems first with tape and then wire and then tape again. A boutonniere is easier to pin on if the stem is taped but not necessarily wired.

All flowers must be ripe when cut, which for the cattleya types means leaving them on the plant about four days after the buds crack. Then flowers should be conditioned in water for overnight or several hours before being made up into corsages. If fresh and ripe when cut, and then properly conditioned, they should last well.

You will find a number of corsage designs in YOU CAN GROW ORCHIDS and even those made with other orchids can be copied with cattleya-type flowers.

Arrangements

You need not be a flower arranger to enjoy your orchids in the house. Of course, if yours is a windowsill collection, you have your plants where you can see them. If your orchids are outdoors or in a greenhouse, you can bring pots of blooming plants into the house, cover the pots, and have ready-made bouquets on the plants.

But you can use orchids in all sorts of designs, from the most conventional buxom Victorian bouquets to the most modern psychedellic designs. Orchids are appropriate and elegant anywhere flowers are used.

THE LANGUAGE OF ORCHIDS

AGAR — A jelly-like nutrient mixture on which seeds are planted in bottles.

ANTHER — The pollen-bearing part of the stamen.

ANEUPLOID — A plant with uneven chromosome number.

ASEXUAL — Propagated without sex, thus not from seed.

BACK BULBS — The rear, old pseudobulbs of a sympodial orchid plant. May be cut off and grown into a separate plant.

BARK — A potting material of dried tree bark.

BIFOLIATE — Plant with more than one leaf per pseudobulb.

BIGENERIC — A hybrid with two genera in its parentage.

BINOMIAL — Two names, genus and species.

BLIND — A pseudobulb lacking flower sheath or flowers.

BULB — Pseudobulb.

CHLOROPHYLL — Green pigment in plant tissue capable of absorbing light.

CHROMOSOME — A microscopic body in a cell which contains the hereditary material (genes).

CLONE — Individual plant and all of its asexually propagated divisions.

COLUMN — A structure formed by the combined sexual parts in a flower.

COMMUNITY POT — Group of identical small seedlings planted in one container.

CONTACT INSECTICIDE — One that kills when sprayed or dusted on the insect or when he touches it.

CROCK — Pieces of broken flower pots, pebbles or other objects placed in bottom of pot below medium to facilitate drainage.

CROSS — (Verb) Transfer of pollen from one flower to another. (Noun) Hybrid from seed produced by two unlike parents.

CULTIVAR — Variety produced in cultivation.

CYTOLOGY — The study of cells.

DIPLOID — Plant with normal basic chromosome number for the species. (Abbreviated 2n).

DIVISION — A piece of a plant.

DORSAL — Refers to the dorsal sepal which is at the top of the flower.

ENVIRONMENT — Grand total of conditions.

EPIPHYTE — Air plant which perches on the surface of another plant but takes no nourishment from the host.

EPITHET — A word or phrase describing a characteristic or quality.

EYE — Vegetative bud capable of growing into another pseudobulb.

FIR BARK — A potting material.

FLASK — A bottle in which orchid seeds are sown. (Verb) To sow orchid seeds in a bottle containing agar.

GENE — A self-duplicating unit of inheritance located in a chromosome.

GENERA — Plural of genus.

GENUS — A group of closely related species. Plural is genera.

GERMINATION — A phase of plant development in which an individual emerges from an embryo or seed.

GREEN POD CULTURE — A method of harvesting and planting orchid seed before the pod matures and splits but when the embryos are capable of developing into plants.

GREX — Latin word for flock. All the seedlings grown from one pod.

HABITAT — Environment or site in which the population of a certain plant normally grows wild.

HAPLOID — The basic chromosome number or half the diploid number. Term designating a single set of chromosomes.

HAPUU — Tree fern fiber used for potting.

HETEROZYGOUS — Possessing unlike genes in the chromosomes.

HEXAPLOID — Having six sets of chromosomes (6n.)

HOMOZYGOUS — Having identical genes in the chromosome pairs.

HUMIDITY — Water vapor content of the atmosphere.

HYBRID — Plant with unlike parents.

INFLORESCENCE — The flowering part of a plant. The arrangement of the flowers on the plant.

INTERSPECIFIC — Hybrid between species.

INTERGENERIC — Hybrid between genera.

KEIKI — Offset, adventitious plantlet.

LABELLUM — One petal different from the other two. Lip.

LABIATE — Alluding to lip, used to describe the group of cattleyas having large lips.

LATERAL — From the sides, applies to the two lower sepals.

LEACH — Wash out.

LEAD — New growth on a sympodial plant.

LIP — Labellum.

LITHOPHYTE — Plant that grows on rock.

MERICLONE — Plant propagated from a meristem.

MERISTEM — Tissue at the growing point of a plant. (Verb) To propagate plants from the meristem tissue.

MULTIGENERIC — Plant having more than two genera in its ancestry. Also called "conglomerate" in this book.

NECTARY — Gland in the flower which secretes sugar substance (nectar) which attracts insects.

NEW JERSEY MIX — A potting medium. See Chapter VII.

NUTRIENTS — Raw materials in soluble form important to plant growth.

OFF MIX — A a potting mixture. See Chapter VII.

OSMUNDA — Fern root used for potting.

OVARY — The part of the flower which develops into the seed pod (fruit).

PEDICEL — Stalk of individual flower. Looks like part of the stem. In cattleyas it contains the ovary.

PENTAPLOID — Having five sets of chromosomes (5n).

PETAL — Three flower parts on orchids, one modified into the lip.

pH — A measure of acidity or alkalinity.

PHOTOSYNTHESIS — Process by which green plants manufacture sugar.

PISTIL — Female element of a flower. Consists of ovary, style, stigma.

POLLEN, POLLINIUM, POLLINIA — Powder or grains, the male element in the fertilization process.

POLLINATE — To transfer pollen from anther to stigma.

POLYPLOID — Having one or more extra sets of chromosomes above the diploid number.

PROTOCORM — Mass of green cells not yet differentiated into plant parts.

PSEUDOBULB — Thickened stem in an orchid plant.

RECESSIVE — Genes for a factor that is suppressed by dominant genes.

RESPIRATION — Process which releases carbon dioxide and water formed by oxidation.

RESUPINATION — Twisting of the flower bud to an inverted position.

RHIZOME — A creeping stem which sends up green parts and sends down roots. The connecting links between the pseudobulbs.

ROSTELLUM — Part of the stigma which separates the anther from the functional stigma to prevent self-pollination.

RUPICOLOUS — Growing on rock.

SARONG — Technically eight leaves covering a pseudobulb which do not develop into functional leaves. See Chapter I.

SEEDLING — A plant grown from seed younger than flowering size or blooming for the first time.

SELF, SELFED, SELFING — Self-fertilization of a flower by its own pollen or that of another flower of the clone.

SEMI-ALBA — Cattleya-type flowers with white sepals and petals except for the lip, which is purple. Also called white-colored-lip.

SEPAL — Outer segments of the flower, three of them.

SHEATH — Protective envelope that encloses young buds.

SPECIES — A group of plants in a genus that are alike. The word is both singular and plural: "A species." "Several species." Do not say "A specie."

STAMEN — The male element of the flower that bears the pollen.

STIGMA — The part of the female element of the flower which receives the pollen.

STYLE — Connecting stalk between stigma and ovary.

SYMPODIAL — Form of growth. See Chapter I.

SYSTEMIC INSECTICIDE — A chemical which penetrates plant tissue and poisons insects which suck or chew that plant.

TEPALS — Sepals and petals of uniform color, excluding the lip.

TERETE — Round. Applies to foliage of some orchids.

TETRAPLOID — Having four sets of chromosomes (4n).

TRANSPIRE — Escape of water vapor through the leaf.

TREE FERN — Fiber for potting.

TRIPLOID — Having three sets of chromosomes (3n).

UNIFOLIATE — Having one leaf per pseudobulb.

VARIETY — A species with some characteristic different from typical form of that species. Abbreviated var. See Chapter V.

VEGETATIVE PROPAGATION — Multiplication without sex, not from seed. See: division, back bulb, meristem.

Lc. Western Sunşet.

GENUS NAMES

Hybrids between genera are becoming so complicated that it is often impossible to guess the make-up of a hybrid by its name. Brassocattleya is obviously Brassavola X Cattleya, but you have no clue as to the genera combined in Fujiwarara.

The following list of conglomerates contains the recognized compound names of hybrids through 1967. However, more new combinations are being named all the time and you can add those that interest you as they appear in the Orchid Review or the American Orchid Society Bulletin.

The Sander's Hybrid Lists (See book list) contain the lists of genera that have registrations in each addendum arranged by the compound name but also by the components, so you can look up Brassavola X Cattleya x Sophronitis under any of these three to find out that the combination is named Rolfeara.

Use the following list for reference. No need to memorize it, but if you know which genera are included in the parentage of each of your plants, you will understand better their needs and care. The name of the genus, whether natural or compound, appears in the first column in capital letters followed by the genera that are in its ancestry. The abbreviations are in parentheses.

ARIZARA (Ariz.) = Cattleya x Domingoa x Epidendrum

BARDENDRUM (Bard.) = Barkeria x Epidendrum
BARKERIA (Bark.) = Natural genus
BLOOMARA (Blma?) = Broughtonia x Laeliopsis x Tetramicra
BRASSAVOLA (B.) = Natural enus
BRASSOCATTLEYA (Bc.) = Brassavola x Cattleya
BRASSODIACRIUM (Bdia.) = Brassavola x Diacrium
BRASSOEPIDENDRUM (Bepi.) = Brassavola x Epidendrum
BRASSOLAELIA (Bl.) = Brassavola x Laelia
BRASSOLAELIOCATTLEYA (Blc.) = Brassavola x Laelia x Cattleya
BRASSOPHRONITIS (Bnts.) = Brassavola x Sophronitis (Syn: SOPHROVOLA)
BRASSOTONIA (Bstna.) = Brassavola x Broughtonia
BROUGHTONIA (Bro.) = Natural genus
BROUGHTOPSIS = Broughtonia x Laeliopsis

CATTLEYA (C.) = Natural genus
CATTLEYOPSIS (Ctps.) = Natural genus
CATTLEYOPSISTONIA (Ctpsta.) = Cattleyopsis x Broughtonia
CATTLEYTONIA (Ctna.) = Cattleya x Broughtonia

DEKENSARA (Dek.) = Brassavola x Cattleya x Schomburgkia
DIABROUGHTONIA (Diab.) = Diacrium x Broughtonia
DIACATTLEYA (Dc.) = Diacrium x Cattleya
DIACRIUM (Diacm.) = Natural genus
DIALAELIA (Dial.) = Diacrium x Laelia
DIALAELIOCATTLEYA (Dlc.) = Diacrium x Laelia x Cattleya
DIALAELIOPSIS (Dialps.) = Diacrium x Laeliopsis
DILLONARA (Dill.) = Epidendrum x Laelia x Schomburkgia
DOMINDESMIA (Ddma.) = Domingoa x Hexadesmia
DOMINGOA (Dga.) = Natural genus
DOMLIOPSIS (Dmlps.) = Domingoa x Laeliopsis

EPIBROUGHTONIA = Epidendrum x Broughtonia (Syn: EPITONIA)
EPICATTLEYA (Epc.) = Epidendrum x Cattleya
EPIDENDRUM (Epi.) = Natural genus
EPIDIACRIUM (Epdcm.) = Epidendrum x Diacrium
EPIGOA (Epg.) = Epidendrum x Domingoa
EPILAELIA (Epl.) = Epidendrum x Laelia
EPILAELIOCATTLEYA (Eplc.) = Epidendrum x Laelia x Cattleya
EPILAELIOPSIS (Eplps.) = Epidendrum x Laeliopsis (Syn: EPILOPSIS)
EPILOPSIS = Epidendrum x Laeliopsis (Syn: EPILAELIOPSIS)
EPIPHRONITELLA = Epidendrum x Sophronitella
EPIPHRONITIS (Ephs.) = Epidendrum x Sophronitis

FUJIWARARA (Fjw.) = Brassavola x Cattleya x Laeliopsis (Syn: TENRAN-
ARA)

GAUNTLETTARA (Gtra.) = Broughtonia x Cattleyopsis x Laeliopsis

HARTARA (Hart.) = Broughtonia x Laelia x Sophronitis

HEXADESMIA (Hex.) = Natural genus
HOOKERARA (Hook.) = Brassavola x Cattleya x Diacrium

IWANAGARA (Iwan.) = Brassavola x Cattleya x Diacrium x Laelia

KIRCHARA (Kir.) = Cattleya x Epidendrum x Laelia x Sophronitis

LAELIA (L.) = Natural genus
LAELIOCATTKERIA (Lcka.) = Laelia x Cattleya x Barkeria
LAELIOCATTLEYA (Lc.) = Laelia x Cattleya
LAELIOPLEYA (Lpya.) = Laeliopsis x Cattleya
LAELIOPSIS (Lps.) = Natural genus
LAELONIA (Lna.) = Laelia x Broughtonia
LAEOPSIS = Laelia x Laeliopsis
LEPTOLAELIA (Lptl.) = Leptotes x Laelia
LEPTOTES (Lpt.) = Natural genus
LOWARA (Low.) = Brassavola x Laelia x Sophronitis

MIZUTARA (Miz.) = Cattleya x Diacrium x Schomburgkia

OSMENTARA (Osmt.) = Broughtonia x Cattleya x Laeliopsis

POTINARA (Pot.) = Brassavola x Cattleya x Laelia x Sophronitis

RECCHARA (Recc.) = Brassavola x Cattleya x Laelia x Schomburgkia
ROLFEARA (Rolf.) = Brassavola x Cattleya x Sophronitis

SCHOMBAVOLA (Smbv.) = Brassavola x Schomburgkia
SCHOMBOCATTLEYA (Smbc.) = Schomburgkia x Cattleya
SCHOMBODIACRIUM (Smbdcm.) = Schomburgkia x Diacrium
SCHOMBOEPIDENDRUM (Smbep.) = Schomburgkia x Epidendrum
SCHOMBOLAELIA (Smbl.) = Schomburgkia x Laelia
SCHOMBOLAELIOCATTLEYA (Smblc.) = Schomburgkia x Laelia x Cattleya
SCHOMBOTONIA = Schomburgkia x Broughtonia
SCHOMBURGKIA (Schom.) = Natural genus
SHIPMANARA (Shipm.) = Broughtonia x Diacrium x Schomburgkia
SOPHROCATTLEYA (Sc.) = Sophronitis x Cattleya
SOPHROLAELIA (Sl.) = Sophronitis x Laelia
SOPHROLAELIOCATTLEYA (Slc.) = Sophronitis x Laelia x Cattleya
SOPHRONITELLA = Natural genus
SOPHRONITIS (Soph.) = Natural genus
SOPHROVOLA = Brassavola x Sophronitis (Syn: BRASSOPHRONITIS)

TETRALIOPSIS (Ttps.) = Tetramicra x Laeliopsis
TETRAMICRA (Ttma.) = Natural genus
TETRATONIA (Ttna.) = Tetramicra x Broughtonia

VAUGHNARA (Vnra.) = Brassavola x Cattleya x Epidendrum

YAMADARA (Yam.) = Brassavola x Cattleya x Epidendrum x Laelia

Cattleya aurantiaca has very small orange flowers, often cupped.

Laelia anceps produces starry flowers on long stems.

INDEX

Pure white form, Cattleya gigas alba 'Lalinde.'

Semi-alba form of C. gigas, white with purple lip.

Colombia, South America, is the home of Cattleya gigas (warsce-wiczii), and in the spring the city of Medellin is an orchid grower's dream because of all the blooms. In addition to cattleyas there are many other genera that are native to and cultivated in the area.

A private collection of cattleyas in Medellin.

Plants of Cattleya gigas naturalized on stumps in a Medellin garden.